Meeting SEN
in the Curriculum:
ART

Other titles in the *Meeting Special Needs in the Curriculum* series:

Meeting Special Needs in English
Tim Hurst
1 84312 157 3

Meeting Special Needs in Maths
Brian Sharp
1 84312 158 1

Meeting Special Needs in Science
Carol Holden and Andy Cooke
1 84312 159 X

Meeting Special Needs in ICT
Michael North and Sally McKeown
1 84312 160 3

Meeting Special Needs in Geography
Diane Swift
1 84312 162 X

Meeting Special Needs in History
Richard Harris and Ian Luff
1 84312 163 8

Meeting Special Needs in PE and Sport
Crispin Andrews
1 84312 164 6

Meeting Special Needs in Modern Foreign Languages
Sally McKeown
1 84312 165 4

Meeting Special Needs in Design and Technology
Louise T. Davies
1 84312 166 2

Meeting Special Needs in Religious Education
Dilwyn Hunt
1 84312 167 0

Meeting Special Needs in Music
Victoria Jaquiss and Diane Paterson
1 84312 168 9

Meeting Special Needs in Citizenship
Alan Combes
1 84312 169 7

Meeting SEN
in the Curriculum:

ART

Kim Earle and Gill Curry

 **David Fulton** Publishers

This book is dedicated to Obi, Maya and Ariki –
future young artists of the twenty-first century.

David Fulton Publishers Ltd
The Chiswick Centre, 414 Chiswick High Road, London W4 5TF

www.fultonpublishers.co.uk

David Fulton Publishers is a division of Granada Learning Limited, part of ITV plc.

10 9 8 7 6 5 4 3 2 1

Note: The right of Kim Earle and Gill Curry to be identified as the authors of this work has been asserted by them in accordance with the Copyright, Designs and Patents Act 1988.

British Library Cataloguing in Publication Data
A catalogue record for this book is available from the British Library.

ISBN 1 84312 161 1

Typeset by Servis Filmsetting Ltd, Manchester
Printed and bound in Great Britain

Contents

Foreword

Art is a creative manifestation of our humanity and our culture, and is fundamental to communicating the human condition. Art in all its forms – from traditional painting and sculpture to more contemporary media such as sound and installation – can absorb us physically, intellectually and emotionally, whether we are experiencing it or making it. The act of creating something new in the world or new to the individual is part of a process that involves imagination, inspiration, curiosity, hypothesising, making, testing and reflection. These are activities common to all of us, young and not so young, and are essential components in the teaching, learning and making of art and our critical engagement with it.

In art, the sharing of ideas through materials and processes, objects and dialogue allows us all points of connection and exchange. Meaning is negotiable; it can be shared or personal. It can coincide with the artist's intention as well as diverge from it. This acceptance of difference is fundamental to the teaching of art, the critical reading of art, the making of art and learning about art.

The authors recognise that every child is an individual, with different ways of seeing the world and being part of it; that every child matters and that every child is entitled to a creative cultural experience. Gill and Kim have written an inspirational and practical book; one that opens up a myriad possibilities for teachers to adapt and develop ideas to suit individual needs and circumstances. It combines sound SEN expertise with subject knowledge in art. Promoting an inclusive, whole-school approach, it provides strategies to support teachers in writing policy for teaching and learning in art and for putting that policy into practice. The book gives advice on creating an inclusive and creative learning environment in the classroom where children and teachers are inspired. There are eight actual case studies of pupils with SEN in real art classrooms. There is advice on working with artists to share ideas and skills, and on understanding their needs and the real benefit of their contribution in the classroom. There is also a recognition that the contemporary artist's practice has embraced new technologies in very exciting ways, and this can produce high-quality, personalised art works that children can be proud of. The use of ICT is explored as a tool and also as a material in making art with pupils with a range of special needs.

The book contains support and advice, project templates, monitoring and assessment guidelines, resources and a comprehensive bibliography – in fact everything you need to know to make a real difference to the teaching and learning of all pupils in our schools through art.

Lindsey Fryer
Head of Interpretation & Education
Tate Liverpool
June 2005

Acknowledgements

We are indebted to the following people and organisations who have helped us to compile this book:

Wirral Education Authority and St Helens Education Authority. Staff and pupils in secondary and primary schools in both LEAs, in particular Pensby High School for Girls and Haydock High School; Mick Carolan at The Hurst School and Orretts Meadow School; Kevin Kelly at St Aelred's Catholic Technology College. Also digital artist Dorrie Halliday.

The National Museums and Galleries on Merseyside, Wirral Museums, the Education Department of Tate Liverpool, Drumcroon, Wigan Education Art Centre and the Royal Academy Outreach Team.

Photographs of the art projects were taken at the following schools and colleges as part of a Wirral-wide LEA Art & Architecture Project in 2000, and we are grateful to the staff and pupils of the schools for permission to include the images:

- Wing Sculpture, Pensby High School for Girls.

- Iron Man wire sculptures, Dawpool Primary School.

- Plates and Portraiture, Cheshire Schools Exhibition, Winsford Lodge School, Cheshire.

- Masks, St Benedict's High School, Wirral, and Pensby High School for Girls.

- Forms in a Landscape, Wirral Teachers Art Workshop 2000.

- Water, Blue Box, Wirral Foundation Student, Wirral Metropolitan College.

- Selection of images from various projects at The Hurst School, St Helens 2003/4.

The following documents have been referred to in our research:

The Cheshire Scheme of Work 1998.

Inside Outside: An Art Resource Pack, Wirral LEA 2000.

The National Curriculum Handbook for Secondary Teachers, DfEE QCA.

Literacy in Art and Design – Writing 2002, Standards and Effectiveness Unit.

The poem 'Musée des Beaux Arts' by W.H. Auden (p.84) is reproduced by permission of: Curtis Brown Ltd, NY; Random House, Inc., NY (N. America); Faber and Faber Ltd, London (UK).

Contributors to the Series

The authors

Kim Earle is currently Able Pupils and Arts Consultant for St Helens LEA on Merseyside. She was formerly a Secondary Head of Art with responsibility for the inclusive teaching of pupils with SEN within the department. She has since worked with students from a variety of special schools on arts initiatives aimed at delivering quality activities to pupils with specific needs to ensure they benefit fully from all that art and design can offer both outside and within the classroom.

Gill Curry is at present Art Consultant for Wirral Education Authority. She was Head of Art and Design in a secondary school, and Head of an Arts Faculty in Wirral for 20 years. Between 1998 and 2000 she worked as Art Advisory Teacher and until 2004 was Gifted and Talented Strand Co-ordinator for Wirral Education Authority. She is a practising artist, specialising in print, and currently studying for an MA in Artist Practice.

A dedicated team of SEN specialists and subject specialists have contributed to the *Meeting Special Needs in the Curriculum Series*.

Series editor

Alan Combes started teaching in South Yorkshire in 1967 and was head of English at several secondary schools before taking on the role of Head of PSHE as part of being senior teacher at Pindar School, Scarborough. He took early retirement to focus on his writing career and has authored two citizenship textbooks as well as writing several features for the *TES*. He has been used as an adviser on citizenship by the DfES and has emphasised citizenship's importance for pupils with special needs as a speaker for NASEN.

SEN specialists

Sue Briggs is a freelance education consultant based in Hereford. She writes and speaks on inclusion, special educational needs and disability, and Autistic Spectrum Disorders and is a lay member of the SEN and Disability Tribunal. Until recently, she was SEN Inclusion Co-ordinator for Herefordshire Education Directorate. Originally trained as a secondary music teacher, Sue has extensive experience in mainstream and special schools. For six years she was teacher in charge of a language disorder unit.

Sue Cunningham is a Learning Support Co-ordinator at a large mainstream secondary school in the West Midlands where she manages a large team of Learning Support teachers and assistants. She has experience of working in both mainstream and special schools and has set up and managed a resource base for pupils with moderate learning difficulties in the mainstream as part of an initiative to promote a more inclusive education for pupils with SEN.

Sally McKeown has responsibility for language-based work in the Inclusion team at BECTA. She has a particular interest in learning difficulties and dyslexia. She wrote the MFL Special Needs Materials for CILT's NOF training and is author of *Unlocking Potential* and co-author of *Supporting Children with Dyslexia* (Questions Publishing). She writes regularly for the *TES, Guardian* and *Special Children* magazines.

Subject specialists

Maths

Brian Sharp is a Key Stage 3 Mathematics consultant for Herefordshire. Brian has a long experience of working both in special and mainstream schools as a teacher of mathematics. He has a range of management experience, including SENCO, mathematics and ICT co-ordinator.

English

Tim Hurst has been a special educational needs co-ordinator in five schools and is particularly interested in the role and use of language in teaching.

Science

Carol Holden works as a science teacher and assistant SENCO in a mainstream secondary school. She has developed courses for pupils with SEN within science and has gained a graduate diploma and MA in Educational Studies, focusing on SEN.

Andy Cooke was a secondary science teacher for 14 years, during which time he has been a Key Stage 3 Science Co-ordinator, Head of Physics and Head of Science. His experience includes teaching in a school with a specialist visually impaired unit. He is currently Science Adviser for Herefordshire. Other publications under his belt include Cambridge University Press's 'Spectrum' series.

History

Richard Harris has been teaching since 1989. He has taught in three comprehensive schools, as history teacher, Head of Department and Head of Faculty. He has also worked as teacher consultant for secondary history in West Berkshire.

Ian Luff is Assistant Headteacher of Kesgrave High School, Suffolk and has been Head of History in three comprehensive schools.

Design and technology

Louise T. Davies is Principal Officer for Design and Technology at the Qualifications and Curriculum Authority and also a freelance consultant. She is an experienced presenter and author of award-winning resources and books for schools. She chairs the Special Needs Advisory Group for the Design and Technology Association.

Religious education

Dilwyn Hunt has worked as a specialist RE adviser, first in Birmingham and now in Dudley. He has a wide range of experience in the teaching of RE, including mainstream and special RE.

Music

Victoria Jaquiss is SEN specialist for music for children with emotional and behavioural difficulties in Leeds. She devised a system of musical notation primarily for use with steel pans, for which, in 2002, she was awarded the fellowship of the Royal Society of Arts.

Diane Paterson works as an inclusive music curriculum teacher in Leeds.

Geography

Diane Swift is a project leader for the Geographical Association. Her interest in special needs developed while she was a Staffordshire geography adviser and inspector.

PE and sport

Crispin Andrews is an education/sports writer with nine years' experience of teaching and sports coaching.

ICT

Mike North works for ICTC, an independent consultancy specialising in the effective use of ICT in education. He develops educational materials and provides advice and support for the SEN sector.

Sally McKeown is an Education Officer with BECTA, the government funded agency responsible for managing the National Grid for Learning and the FERL website. She is responsible for the use of IT for learners and disabilities, learning difficulties or additional needs.

Citizenship

Alan Combes started teaching in South Yorkshire in 1967 and was Head of English at several secondary schools before taking on the role of Head of PSHE as part of being senior teacher at Pindar School, Scarborough. He took early retirement to focus on his writing career and has authored two citizenship textbooks as well as writing several features for the *TES*. He has been used as an adviser on citizenship by the DfES and has emphasised citizenship's importance for special needs pupils as a speaker for NASEN.

Modern foreign languages

Sally McKeown is responsible for language-based work in the Inclusion team at BECTA. She has a particular interest in learning difficulties and dyslexia. She writes regularly for the *TES, Guardian,* and *Special Children* magazine.

Contents of the CD

The CD contains activities and record sheets that can be amended/individualised and printed out for use by the purchasing institution.

Please note that some of the images in the book have been included on the CD to allow readers to print out in full colour.

Increasing the font size and spacing will improve accessibility for some students, as will changes in background colour. Alternatively, print onto pastel-coloured paper for greater ease of reading.

Images:

Iron man
Forms in Landscapes
Picasso plates and portraiture
Identity
Flight
Water

Introduction

> All children have the right to a good education and the opportunity to fulfil their potential. All teachers should expect to teach children with special educational needs (SEN) and all schools should play their part in educating children from the local community, whatever their background or ability. (*Removing Barriers to Achievement: The Government's Strategy for SEN, 2004*)

A raft of legislation and statutory guidance over the past few years has sought to make our mainstream education system more inclusive and ensure that pupils with a diverse range of ability and need are well catered for. This means that all staff need to have an awareness of how children learn and develop in different ways and an understanding of how barriers to achievement can be removed – or at least minimised.

These barriers often result from inappropriate teaching styles, inaccessible teaching materials or ill-advised grouping of pupils, as much as from an individual child's physical, sensory or cognitive impairments: a fact that is becoming better understood. It is this developing understanding that is now shaping the legislative and advisory landscape of our education system, and exhorting all teachers to carefully consider their curriculum planning and classroom practice.

The major statutory requirements and non-statutory guidance are summarised in Chapter 1, setting the context for this resource and providing useful starting points for departmental INSET.

It is clear that provision for pupils with special educational needs is not the sole responsibility of the special educational needs co-ordinator (SENCO) and her/his team of assistants. If, in the past, subject teachers have 'taken a back seat' in the planning and delivery of a suitable curriculum for these children and expected the Learning Support department to bridge the gap between what was on offer in the classroom, lab or studio and what they actually needed, they can no longer do so.

> All teaching and non teaching staff should be involved in the development of the school's SEN policy and be fully aware of the school's procedure for identifying, assessing and making provision for pupils with SEN. (Table of Roles and Responsibilities, Code of Practice, 2001)

Chapter 2 looks at departmental policy for SEN provision and provides useful audit material for reviewing and developing current practice.

The term 'special educational needs' or SEN is now widely used and has become something of a catch-all descriptor – rendering it less than useful in many cases. Before the Warnock Report (1978) and subsequent introduction of the term 'special educational needs', any pupils who for whatever reason (cognitive difficulties, emotional and behavioural difficulties, speech and language disorders) progressed more slowly than the 'norm' were designated 'remedials' and grouped together in the bottom sets, without the benefit, in many cases, of specialist subject teachers.

But the SEN tag was also applied to pupils in special schools who had more significant needs and had previously been identified as 'disabled' or even 'uneducable'. Add to these the deaf pupils, those with impaired vision, others with mobility problems, and even children from other countries with a limited understanding of the English language – who may or may not have been highly intelligent – and you have a recipe for confusion to say the least.

The day-to-day descriptors used in the staffroom are gradually being moderated and refined as greater knowledge and awareness of special needs is built up. (We still hear staff describing pupils as 'totally thick', a 'nutcase' or 'complete moron' – but hopefully only as a means of letting off steam!) However, there are terms in common use which, though more measured and well-meaning, can still be unhelpful and misleading. Teachers will describe a child as being 'dyslexic' when they mean that he is poor at reading and writing; 'ADHD' has become a synonym for badly behaved; and a child who seems to be withdrawn or just eccentric is increasingly described as 'autistic'.

The whole process of applying labels is fraught with danger, but sharing a common vocabulary – and more importantly, a common understanding – can help colleagues to express their concerns about a pupil and address the issues as they appear in the art room. Often, this is better achieved by identifying the particular areas of difficulty experienced by the pupil rather than puzzling over what syndrome he/she may have. The Code of Practice identifies four main areas of difficulty and these are detailed in Chapter 3 – along with an 'at a glance' guide to a wide range of syndromes and conditions and guidance on how they might present barriers to learning.

There is no doubt that the number of children with special needs being educated in mainstream schools is growing:

> . . . because of the increased emphasis on the inclusion of children with SEN in mainstream schools the number of these children is increasing, as are the severity and variety of their SEN. Children with a far wider range of learning difficulties and variety of medical conditions, as well as sensory difficulties and physical disabilities, are now attending mainstream classes. The implication of that is that mainstream school teachers need to expand their knowledge and skills with regard to the needs of children with SEN. (Stakes and Hornby 2000:3)

The continuing move to greater inclusion means that all teachers can now expect to teach pupils with varied, and quite significant special educational needs at some time. Even five years ago, it was rare to come across children with Asperger's/Down's/Tourette's Syndrome, Autistic Spectrum Disorder or significant physical/sensory disabilities in community secondary schools. Now, they are entering mainstream education in growing numbers and there is a realisation that their 'inclusion' cannot be simply the responsibility of the SENCO and support staff. All staff have to be aware of particular learning needs and able to employ strategies in the classroom (and lab, studio, gym) that directly address those needs.

Chapter 4 considers the aspects of art and design provision that can benefit the pupil with SEN. It examines the aims of art education and a variety of differentiation methods, leading onto effective planning that includes working with artists-in-residence, the use of sketchbooks and the physical environment of the artroom. The key areas that need to be considered when developing or reviewing an inclusive art policy are discussed.

Chapter 5 contains Key Stage 3 art and design projects for pupils with SEN.

Chapter 6 looks at a number of case studies with some exemplar projects and materials. Describing real life situations with real pupils is a powerful way to demonstrate ideas and guidance.

Chapter 7 provides exemplar materials on monitoring and assessment in the art and design department. These are generic documents taken from a mainstream school but do provide a strong basis for planning and provision that can be adapted according to the needs of the students in your school.

The revised regulations for SEN provision make it clear that mainstream schools are expected to provide for pupils with a wide diversity of needs, and teaching is evaluated on the extent to which all pupils are engaged and enabled to achieve. This book has been produced in response to the implications of all of this for secondary subject teachers. It has been written by subject specialists with support from colleagues who have expertise within the SEN field so that the information and guidance given is both subject-specific and pedagogically sound. The book and accompanying CD provide a resource that can be used with colleagues:

- to shape departmental policy and practice for special needs provision;

- to enable staff to react with a measured response when inclusion issues arise;

- to ensure that every pupil achieves appropriately in art.

CHAPTER 1

Meeting Special Educational Needs – Your Responsibility

Inclusion in education involves the process of increasing the participation of students in, and reducing their exclusion from, the cultures, curricula and communities of local schools. (*Index for Inclusion* 2000)

The *Index for Inclusion* was distributed to all maintained schools by the Department for Education and Skills and has been a valuable tool for many schools as they have worked to develop their inclusive practice. It supports schools in the review of their policies, practices and procedures, and the development of an inclusive approach. Where it has been used as part of the school improvement process – looking at inclusion in the widest sense – it has been a great success. For many people, however, the *Index* lacked any real teeth and recent legislation and non-statutory guidance is more authoritative.

The SEN and Disability Act 2001 (SENDA)

The Act amended the Disability Discrimination Act and created important new duties for schools:

- to take reasonable steps to ensure that disabled pupils are not placed at a substantial disadvantage in relation to the education and other services they provide. This means they must anticipate where barriers to learning lie and take action to remove them as far as they are able;

- to plan strategically to increase the extent to which disabled pupils can participate in the curriculum, make the physical environment more accessible and ensure that written material is provided in accessible formats.

The reasonable steps taken might include:

- changing policies and practices
- changing course requirements

- changing physical features of a building

- providing interpreters or other support workers

- delivering courses in alternative ways

- providing materials in other formats

See Chapter 2 for further detail on SENDA and an INSET activity.

The Revised National Curriculum

The Revised National Curriculum (2002) emphasises the provision of effective learning opportunities for all learners and establishes three principles for promoting inclusion:

- the setting of suitable learning challenges

- responding to pupils' diverse learning needs

- overcoming potential barriers to learning and assessment

The National Curriculum guidance suggests that staff may need to differentiate tasks and materials, and facilitate access to learning by:

- encouraging pupils to use all available senses and experiences;

- planning for participation in all activities;

- helping children to manage their behaviour, take part in learning and prepare for work;

- helping pupils to manage their emotions;

- giving teachers, where necessary, the discretion to teach pupils material from earlier key stages, providing consideration is given to age-appropriate learning context. (This means that a 14-year-old with significant learning difficulties may be taught relevant aspects of the programmes of study for art at Key Stage 3, but at the same time working on suitable material founded in the Programme of Study for Key Stage 1.)

The Qualifications and Curriculum Authority (QCA) have also introduced performance descriptions (P levels/P scales) to enable teachers to observe and record small steps of progress made by some pupils with SEN. These descriptions outline early learning and attainment for each subject in the National Curriculum, including citizenship, RE and PSHE. They chart progress up to NC level 1 through eight steps. The performance descriptions for P1 to P3 are common across all subjects and outline the types and range of general performance that some pupils with learning difficulties might characteristically demonstrate. From level P4, many believe it is possible to describe performance in a way that indicates the emergence of subject-focused skills, knowledge and understanding.

The Code of Practice for Special Educational Needs

The Revised Code of Practice (implemented in 2002) describes a cyclical process of planning, target setting and review for pupils with special educational needs. It also makes clear the expectation that the vast majority of pupils with special needs will be educated in mainstream settings. Those identified as needing over and above what the school can provide from its own resources, however, are nominated for 'School Action Plus' and outside agencies will be involved in planned intervention. This may involve professionals from the Learning Support Service, a specialist teacher or therapist, or an educational psychologist, working with the school's SENCO to put together an Individual Education Plan (IEP) for the pupil. In a minority of cases (the numbers vary widely between LEAs) pupils may be assessed by a multidisciplinary team on behalf of the local education authority whose representatives then decide whether or not to issue a Statement of SEN. This is a legally binding document detailing the child's needs and setting out the resources that should be provided. It is reviewed every year.

The Fundamental Principles of the *Special Educational Needs Code of Practice* are as follows:

- A child with special educational needs should have their needs met.

- The special educational needs of children will normally be met in mainstream schools or settings.

- The views of the child should be sought and taken into account.

- Parents have a vital role to play in supporting their child's education.

- Children with special educational needs should be offered full access to a broad, balanced and relevant education, including an appropriate curriculum for the foundation stage and the National Curriculum.

Ofsted

Ofsted inspectors are required to make judgements about a school's inclusion policy, and how this is translated into practice in individual classrooms. According to Ofsted (2003), the following key factors help schools to become more inclusive:

- a climate of acceptance of all pupils;

- careful preparation of placements for pupil with SEN;

- availability of sufficient suitable teaching and personal support;

- widespread awareness among staff of the particular needs of SEN pupils and an understanding of the practical ways of meeting these needs in the classroom;

- sensitive allocation to teaching groups and careful curriculum modification, timetables and social arrangements;

- availability of appropriate materials and teaching aids and adapted accommodation;

- an active approach to personal and social development, as well as to learning;

- well-defined and consistently applied approaches to managing difficult behaviour;

- assessment, recording and reporting procedures which can embrace and express adequately the progress of pupils with more complex SEN who make only small gains in learning and PSD;

- involving parents/carers as fully as possible in decision-making, keeping them well informed about their child's progress and giving them as much practical support as possible;

- developing and taking advantage of training opportunities, including links with special schools and other schools.

Policy into practice

Effective teaching for pupils with special educational needs is, by and large, effective for all pupils, but as schools become more inclusive, teachers need to be able to respond to a wider range of needs. The Government's strategy for SEN (*Removing Barriers to Achievement*, 2004) sets out ambitious proposals to 'help teachers expand their repertoire of inclusive skills and strategies and plan confidently to include children with increasingly complex needs'.

In many cases, pupils' individual needs will be met through greater differentiation of tasks and materials, i.e. school-based intervention as set out in the *SEN Code of Practice*. A smaller number of pupils may need access to specialist equipment and approaches or to alternative or adapted activities, as part of a 'School Action Plus' programme, augmented by advice and support from external specialists. The QCA give the following guidance on their website (2003). Teachers are encouraged to take specific action to provide access to learning for pupils with special educational needs by:

(a) Providing for pupils who need help with communication, language and literacy, through:

  - using texts that pupils can read and understand;

  - using visual and written materials in different formats, including large print, symbol text and braille;

  - using ICT, other technological aids and taped materials;

- using alternative and augmentative communication, including signs and symbols;

- using translators, communicators and amanuenses.

(b) Planning, where necessary, to develop pupils' understanding through the use of all available senses and experiences:

- using materials and resources that pupils can access through sight, touch, sound, taste or smell;

- using word descriptions and other stimuli to make up for a lack of first-hand experiences;

- using ICT, visual and other materials to increase pupils' knowledge of the wider world;

- encouraging pupils to take part in activities such as visits to art galleries and exploring the environment.

(c) Planning for pupils' full participation in learning and in physical and practical activities:

- using specialist aids and equipment;

- providing support from adults or peers when needed;

- adapting tasks or environments;

- providing alternative activities, where necessary.

(d) Helping pupils to manage their behaviour, to take part in learning effectively and safely, and, at Key Stage 4, to prepare for work:

- setting realistic demands and stating them explicitly;

- using positive behaviour management, including a clear structure of rewards and sanctions;

- giving pupils every chance and encouragement to develop the skills they need to work well with a partner or a group;

- teaching pupils to value and respect the contribution of others;

- encouraging and teaching independent working skills;

- teaching essential safety rules.

(e) Helping individuals to manage their emotions, particularly trauma or stress, and to take part in learning:

- identifying aspects of learning in which the pupil will engage and planning short-term, easily achievable goals in selected activities;

- providing positive feedback to reinforce and encourage learning and build self-esteem;

- selecting tasks and materials sensitively to avoid unnecessary stress for the pupil;

- creating a supportive learning environment in which the pupil feels safe and is able to engage with learning;

- allowing time for the pupil to engage with learning and gradually increasing the range of activities and demands.

Pupils with disabilities

Not all pupils with disabilities will necessarily have special educational needs. Many learn alongside their peers with little need for additional resources beyond the aids that they use as part of their daily life, such as a wheelchair, a hearing aid or equipment to aid vision. Teachers' planning must ensure, however, that these pupils are enabled to participate as fully and effectively as possible in the curriculum by:

- Planning appropriate amounts of time to allow for the satisfactory completion of tasks. This might involve:

  - taking account of the very slow pace at which some pupils will be able to record work, either manually or with specialist equipment, and of the physical effort required;

  - being aware of the high levels of concentration necessary for some pupils when following or interpreting text or graphics, particularly when using vision aids or tactile methods, and of the tiredness which may result;

  - allocating sufficient time, opportunity and access to equipment for pupils to gain information through experimental work and detailed observation, including the use of microscopes;

  - being aware of the effort required by some pupils to follow oral work, whether through use of residual hearing, lip reading or a signer, and of the tiredness or loss of concentration which may occur.

- Planning opportunities, where necessary, for the development of skills in practical aspects of the curriculum. This might involve:

  - providing adapted, modified or alternative activities or approaches to learning in art and design, ensuring that these have integrity and equivalence to the National Curriculum and that they enable pupils to make appropriate progress;

  - providing alternative or adapted activities in art and design for pupils who are unable to manipulate tools, equipment or materials or who may be allergic to certain types of materials;

  - ensuring that all pupils can be included and participate safely in visits to museums and galleries, places of interest when sketching outdoors or working with an artist-in-residence.

- Identifying aspects of programmes of study and attainment targets that may present specific difficulties for individuals. This might involve:

  - using approaches to enable hearing impaired pupils to learn about sound representation and cross-curricular aspects in art;

  - helping visually impaired pupils to learn about and evaluate images in art and design;

  - providing opportunities for pupils to develop other strengths where they cannot meet the particular requirements of a subject, such as the visual requirements in art and design;

  - discounting these aspects in appropriate individual cases when required to make a judgement against level descriptions.

The success of art and design

In the National Curriculum Handbook (1999) it states:

> Art and design stimulates creativity and imagination. It provides visual, tactile and sensory experiences and a unique way of understanding and responding to the world. Pupils use colour, form, texture, pattern and different materials and processes to communicate what they see, feel and think.

Art and design for pupils with SEN makes a valuable contribution to the development of their practical, thinking, creative and expressive skills. They can acquire knowledge, skills and understanding through a variety of starting points for practical work including themselves, their own experiences, natural and manmade objects and environments. They may work on their own or in collaboration with others on projects in two or three dimensions and on different scales. They can use a range of materials and approaches (including ICT); for example, painting, collage, printmaking, digital media, textiles and sculpture.

> Art and design is not just a subject to learn, but an activity you can practise: with your hands, your eyes, your whole personality. (Quentin Blake, Children's Laureate).

Summary

Teachers are ultimately responsible for all the children they teach, in terms of participation, achievement, enjoyment. Pupils with a wide range of needs – physical/sensory, emotional, cognitive and social – are present in increasing numbers, in all mainstream settings. Government policies point the way, with inclusion at the forefront of national policy – but it is up to teachers to make the rhetoric a reality.

Departmental Policy

It is crucial that departmental policy describes a strategy for meeting pupils' SEN within the particular curricular area. The policy should set the scene for any visitor to the art department – from supply staff to inspectors – and make a valuable contribution to the departmental handbook. The process of developing a department SEN policy offers the opportunity to clarify and evaluate current thinking and practice within the art team and to establish a consistent approach.

The policy should:

- clarify the responsibilities of all staff and identify any with specialist training and/or knowledge

- define the purpose of art education in the particular setting (see Chapter 4)

- describe the curriculum on offer and how it can be differentiated (with reference to the use of ICT and any specialist equipment)

- outline the strategies used by staff in the department for grouping pupils

- outline arrangements for assessment and reporting and ensuring continuity

- include health and safety issues

- refer to budget and allocation of resources

- give guidance on planning visits to galleries etc

- guide staff on how to work effectively with support staff

- identify staff training

The starting point will be the school's SEN policy as required by the Education Act 1996, with each subject department 'fleshing out' the detail in a way that describes how things work in practice. The writing of a policy should be much more than a paper exercise completed to satisfy the senior management team and Ofsted inspectors: it is an opportunity for staff to come together as a team and create a framework for teaching art in a way that makes it accessible to all pupils in the school.

Where to start when writing a policy

An audit can act as a starting point for reviewing current policy on SEN or can inform the writing of a new policy. It will involve gathering information and reviewing current practice with regard to pupils with SEN and is best completed by the whole of the department, preferably with some additional advice from the SENCO or another member of staff with responsibility for SEN within the school. An audit carried out by the whole department can provide a valuable opportunity for professional development if it is seen as an exercise in sharing good practice and encouraging joint planning. But before embarking on an audit, it is worth investing some time in a department meeting or training day, to raise awareness of special educational needs legislation and establish a shared philosophy. (An INSET activity is provided at the end of this chapter.)

Useful headings when establishing a working policy

General statement

- What does legislation and DfES guidance say?

- What does the school policy state?

- What do members of the department have to do to comply with it?

Definition of SEN

- What does SEN mean?

- What are the areas of need and the categories used in the Code of Practice?

- Are there any special implications within the subject area?

Provision for staff within the department

- Who has responsibility for SEN within the department?

- How and when is information shared?

- Where and what information is stored?

Provision for pupils with SEN

- How are pupils with SEN assessed and monitored in the department?

- How are contributions to IEPs and reviews made?

- What criteria are used for organising teaching groups?

- What alternative courses are offered to pupils with SEN?

- What special internal and external examination arrangements are made?

- What guidance is available for working with support staff?

Resources and learning materials

- Is there any specialist equipment used in the department?

- How are resources developed?

- Where are resources stored?

Staff qualifications and Continuing Professional Development needs

- What qualifications do the members of the department have?

- What training has taken place?

- How is training planned?

- Is a record kept of training completed and training needs?

Monitoring and reviewing the policy

- How will the policy be monitored?

- When will the policy be reviewed?

The content of an SEN departmental policy

This section gives detailed information on what an SEN policy might include. Each heading is expanded with some detailed information and raises the main issues with regard to teaching pupils with SEN. At the end of each section there is an example statement. The example statements can be personalised and brought together to make a policy.

General statement with reference to the school's SEN policy

All schools must have an SEN policy according to the Education Act 1996. This policy will set out basic information on the school's SEN provision, and how the school identifies, assesses and provides for pupils with SEN, including information on staffing and working in partnership with other professionals and parents. Any department policy needs to have reference to the school SEN policy.

Example

> All members of the department will ensure that the needs of all pupils with SEN are met according to the aims of the school and its SEN policy.

Definition of SEN

It is useful to insert at least the four areas of SEN in the department policy, as used in the Code of Practice for Special Educational Needs.

TABLE 2.1 THE FOUR AREAS OF SEN

Cognition and Learning Needs	Behavioural, Emotional and Social Development Needs	Communication and Interaction Needs	Sensory and/ or Physical Needs
Specific learning difficulties (SpLD)	Behavioural, emotional and social difficulties (BESD)	Speech, language and communication needs	Hearing impairment (HI)
Dyslexia			Visual impairment (VI)
Moderate learning difficulties (MLD)	Attention Deficit Disorder (ADD)	Autistic Spectrum Disorder (ASD)	
Severe learning difficulties (SLD)	Attention Deficit Hyperactivity Disorder (ADHD)	Asperger's Syndrome	Multi-sensory impairment (MSI)
Profound and multiple learning difficulties (PMLD)			Physical difficulties (PD)

Provision for staff within the department

In many schools, each department nominates a member of staff to have special responsibility for SEN provision (with or without remuneration). This can be very effective where there is a system of regular liaison between department SEN representatives and the SENCO in the form of meetings or paper communications or a mixture of both.

The responsibilities of this post may include liaison between the department and the SENCO, attending any liaison meetings and providing feedback via meetings and minutes, attending training, maintaining the departmental SEN information and records and representing the needs of pupils with SEN at departmental level. This post can be seen as a valuable development opportunity for staff. The name of this person should be included in the policy.

Setting out how members of the department raise concerns about pupils with SEN can be included in this section. Concerns may be raised at specified departmental meetings before referral to the SENCO. An identified member of the department could make referrals to the SENCO and keep a record of this information.

Reference to working with support staff will include a commitment to planning and communication between staff. There may be information on inviting support staff to meetings, resources and lesson plans.

A reference to the centrally held lists of pupils with SEN and other relevant information will also be included in this section. A note about confidentiality of information should be included.

Example

> The member of staff with responsibility for overseeing the provision of SEN within the department will attend liaison meetings and feed back to other members of the department. He/she will maintain the department's SEN information file, attend appropriate training and disseminate this to all departmental staff. All information will be treated with confidentiality.

Provision for pupils with SEN

It is the responsibility of all staff to know which pupils have SEN and to identify any pupils having difficulties. Pupils with SEN may be identified by staff within the department in a variety of ways, which may be listed and could include:

- observation in lessons
- assessment of class work
- homework tasks
- end of module tests
- progress checks
- annual examinations
- reports

Setting out how pupils with SEN are grouped within the art department may include specifying the criteria used and/or the philosophy behind the method of grouping.

Example

The pupils are taught in mixed ability tutor groups. Monitoring arrangements and details of how pupils can move between groups should also be set out. Information collected may include:

- National Curriculum levels
- departmental assessments
- reading scores
- advice from pastoral staff
- discussion with staff in the SEN department
- information provided on IEPs

Special examination arrangements need to be considered not only at Key Stages 3 and 4 but also for internal examinations. How and when these will be discussed should be clarified. Reference to SENCO and examination arrangements from the examination board should be taken into account. Recognition that staff in the department understand the current legislation and guidance from central government is important, so a reference to the SEN Code of Practice and the levels of SEN intervention is helpful within the policy. Here is a good place also to put a statement about the school behaviour policy, rewards and sanctions, and how the department will make any necessary adjustments to meet the needs of pupils with SEN.

Example

It is understood that pupils with SEN may receive additional support if they have a statement of SEN, are at School Action Plus or School Action. The staff in the art department will aim to support the pupils to achieve their targets as specified on their IEPs and will provide feedback for IEP or statement reviews. Pupils with SEN will be included in the departmental monitoring system used for all pupils. Additional support will be requested as appropriate.

Resources and learning materials

The department policy needs to specify what differentiated materials are available, where they are kept and how to find new resources. This section could include a statement about working with support staff to develop resources or access specialist resources as needed, and the use of ICT. Teaching strategies may also be identified if appropriate. Advice on more specialist equipment can be sought as necessary, possibly through LEA support services: contact details may be available from the SENCO, or the department may have direct links. Any specially bought subject text or alternative/appropriate courses can be specified as well as any external assessment and examination courses.

Example

> The department will provide suitably differentiated materials and, where appropriate, specialist resources for pupils with SEN. Additional texts are available for those pupils working below National Curriculum level 3. At Key Stage 4 an alternative course to GCSE is offered at Entry level but, where possible, pupils with SEN will be encouraged to reach their full potential and follow a GCSE course. Support staff will be provided with curriculum information in advance of lessons and will also be involved in lesson planning. A list of resources is available in the department handbook and on the noticeboard.

Staff qualifications and Continuing Professional Development needs

It is important to recognise and record the qualifications and special skills gained by staff within the department. Training can include not only external courses but also in-house INSET and opportunities such as observing other staff, working to produce materials with other staff and visiting other establishments. Staff may have hidden skills that might enhance the work of the department and the school, for example, some staff might be proficient in the use of sign language.

Example

> A record of training undertaken, specialist skills and training required will be kept in the department handbook. Requests for training will be considered in line with the department and school improvement plan.

Monitoring and reviewing the policy

To be effective any policy needs regular monitoring and review. These can be planned as part of the yearly cycle. The responsibility for the monitoring can rest with the Head of Department but will have more effect if supported by someone from outside acting as a critical friend. This could be the SENCO or a member of the senior management team in school.

Example

> The department SEN policy will be monitored by the Head of Department on a planned annual basis, with advice being sought from the SENCO as part of a three-yearly review process.

Summary

Creating a departmental SEN policy should be a developmental activity to improve the teaching and learning for all pupils but especially those with special or additional needs. The policy should be a working document that will evolve and change; it is there to challenge current practice and to encourage improvement for both pupils and staff. If departmental staff work together to create the policy, they will have ownership of it; it will have true meaning and be effective in clarifying practice.

INSET Activity 1: What do we really think?

Each member of the department should choose two of these statements and pin them onto the noticeboard for an overview of staff opinion. The person leading the session (Head of Department, SENCO or senior manager) should be ready to address any issues and take the department forward in a positive approach.

'If my own child had special needs, I would want her/him to be in a mainstream school mixing with all sorts of kids.'

'I want to be able to cater for pupils with SEN but feel that I don't have the expertise required.'

'Special needs kids in mainstream schools are all right up to a point, but I didn't sign up for dealing with the more severe problems – they should be in special schools.'

'It is the SENCO's responsibility to look out for these pupils with SEN – with help from support teachers.'

'Pupils with special needs should be catered for the same as any others. Teachers can't pick and choose the pupils they want to teach.'

'I need much more time to plan if pupils with SEN are going to be coming to my lessons.'

'Big schools are just not the right places for blind or deaf kids, or those in wheelchairs.'

'I would welcome more training on how to provide for pupils with SEN in my subject.'

'I have enough to do without worrying about kids who can't read or write.'

'If their behaviour distracts other pupils in any way, youngsters with SEN should be withdrawn from the class.'

Different Types of SEN

This chapter is a starting point for information on the special educational needs most frequently occurring in the mainstream secondary school. It describes the main characteristics of each learning difficulty with practical ideas for use in subject areas, and contacts for further information. Some of the tips are based on good secondary practice whilst others encourage teachers to try new or less familiar approaches.

The special educational needs in this chapter are grouped under the headings used in the SEN Code of Practice (DfES 2001):

- cognition and learning

- behaviour, emotional and social development

- communication and interaction

- sensory and/or physical needs

(See Table 2.1 in Chapter 2).

The labels used in this chapter are useful when describing pupils' difficulties but it is important to remember not to use the label in order to define the pupil. Put the pupil before the difficulty, saying 'the pupil with special educational needs' rather than 'the SEN pupil', 'Pupils with MLD' rather than 'MLDs'.

Remember to take care in using labels when talking with parents, pupils or other professionals. Unless a pupil has a firm diagnosis, and parents and pupil understand the implications of that diagnosis, it is more appropriate to describe the features of the special educational need rather than use the label. For example, a teacher might describe a pupil's spelling difficulties but not use the term 'dyslexic'.

The number and profile of pupils with special educational needs will vary from school to school, so it is important to consider the pupil with SEN as an individual within your school and subject environment. The strategies contained in this chapter will help teachers adapt that environment to meet the needs of individual pupils within the subject context. For example, rather than saying, 'He can't read the worksheet', recognise that the worksheet is too difficult for the pupil, and adapt the work accordingly.

There is a continuum of need within each of the special educational needs listed here. Some pupils will be affected more than others, and show fewer or more of the characteristics described.

The availability and levels of support from professionals within a school (e.g. SENCOs, support teachers, teaching assistants) and external professionals (e.g. educational psychologists, Learning Support Service staff, medical staff) will depend on the severity of pupils' SEN. This continuum of need will also impact on the subject teacher's planning and allocation of support staff.

Pupils with other, less common, special educational needs may be included in some secondary schools, and additional information on these conditions may be found in a variety of sources. These include the school SENCO, LEA support services, educational psychologists and the Internet.

Asperger's Syndrome

Asperger's Syndrome is a disorder at the able end of the autistic spectrum. People with Asperger's Syndrome have average to high intelligence but share the same Triad of Impairments. They often want to make friends but do not understand the complex rules of social interaction. They have impaired fine and gross motor skills, with writing being a particular problem. Boys are more likely to be affected – with the ratio being 10:1 boys to girls. Because they appear 'odd' and naïve, these pupils are particularly vulnerable to bullying.

Main characteristics

- **Social interaction**
  Pupils with Asperger's Syndrome want friends but have not developed the strategies necessary for making and sustaining friendships. They find it very difficult to learn social norms and to pick up on social cues. High social situations, such as lessons, can cause great anxiety.

- **Social communication**
  Pupils have appropriate spoken language but tend to sound formal and pedantic, using little expression and with an unusual tone of voice. They have difficulty using and understanding non-verbal language such as facial expression, gesture, body language and eye contact. They have a literal understanding of language and do not grasp implied meanings.

- **Social imagination**
  Pupils with Asperger's Syndrome need structured environments, and to have routines they understand and can anticipate. They excel at learning facts and figures, but have difficulty understanding abstract concepts and in generalising information and skills. They often have all-consuming special interests.

How can the art teacher help?

- Liaise closely with parents, especially over homework.
- Create as calm a classroom environment as possible.
- Allow the pupil to sit in the same place for each lesson.
- Set up a work buddy system for your lessons.
- Provide a variety of visual stimuli in class.
- Give time to process questions and respond.
- Make sure pupils understand what to do.
- Allow many opportunities for direct observation rather than imaginative composition or abstraction.
- Use visual timetables and task activity lists.
- Prepare for changes to routines well in advance; liaise with parents if considering a school visit to a gallery or museum, for example.
- Give written homework instructions and stick into a sketchbook or on the back of a piece of plain paper upon which homework should be completed.
- Have your own class rules and apply them consistently.

The National Autistic Society, 393 City Road, London ECIV 1NG
Tel: 0845 070 4004 Helpline (10 a.m.–4 p.m., Mon–Fri); Tel: 020 7833 2299
Fax: 020 7833 9666
Email: nas@nas.org.uk Website: http://www.nas.org.uk

Attention Deficit Disorder (with or without hyperactivity) (ADD/ADHD)

'Attention Deficit Hyperactivity Disorder' is a term used to describe children who exhibit over-active behaviour and impulsivity and who have difficulty in paying attention. It is caused by a form of brain dysfunction of a genetic nature. ADHD can sometimes be controlled effectively by medication. Children of all levels of ability can have ADHD.

Main characteristics

- difficulty in following instructions and completing tasks
- easily distracted by noise, movement of others, objects attracting attention
- often doesn't listen when spoken to
- fidgets and becomes restless, can't sit still
- interferes with other pupils' work
- can't stop talking, interrupts others, calls out
- runs about when inappropriate
- has difficulty in waiting or taking turns
- acts impulsively without thinking about the consequences

How can the art teacher help?

- Make eye contact and use the pupil's name when speaking to him or her.
- Keep instructions simple – the one sentence rule.
- Demonstrate what you want the pupil to do.
- Provide clear routines and rules, and rehearse them regularly.
- Sit the pupil away from obvious distractions, e.g. windows, store cupboard, computer.
- In busy situations direct the pupil by name to visual or practical objects, materials or tools.
- Encourage the pupil to repeat back instructions before starting work.
- Tell the pupil when to begin a task.
- Give two choices – avoid the option of the pupil saying 'no', by asking, for example, 'Do you want to use pencil or fineliner?'
- Give advanced warning when something is about to happen, change or finish with a time, e.g. 'In two minutes I need you (pupil name) to. . .'
- Give specific praise – catch the pupil being good, give attention for positive behaviour or taking care with work.
- Give the pupil responsibilities so that others can see him in a positive light and he develops a positive self-image, e.g. demonstrate to other pupils how he has done something in his art or craftwork that worked particularly well.

ADD Information Services, PO Box 340, Edgware, Middlesex HA8 9HL
Tel: 020 8906 9068
ADDNET UK Website: www.btinternet.com/~black.ice/addnet/

Autistic Spectrum Disorders (ASD)

The term 'Autistic Spectrum Disorders' is used for a range of disorders affecting the development of social interaction, social communication, and social imagination and flexibility of thought. This is known as the 'Triad of Impairments'. Pupils with ASD cover the full range of ability and the severity of the impairment varies widely. Some pupils also have learning disabilities or other difficulties. Four times as many boys as girls are diagnosed with an ASD.

Main characteristics

- **Social interaction**
  Pupils with an ASD find it difficult to understand social behaviour and this affects their ability to interact with children and adults. They do not always understand social contexts. They may experience high levels of stress and anxiety in settings that do not meet their needs or when routines are changed. This can lead to inappropriate behaviour.

- **Social communication**
  Understanding and use of non-verbal and verbal communication is impaired. Pupils with an ASD have difficulty understanding the communication of others and in developing effective communication themselves. They have a literal understanding of language. Many are delayed in learning to speak, and some never develop speech at all.

- **Social imagination and flexibility of thought**
  Pupils with an ASD have difficulty in thinking and behaving flexibly which may result in restricted, obsessional or repetitive activities. They are often more interested in objects than people, and have intense interests in such things as trains and vacuum cleaners. Pupils work best when they have a routine. Unexpected changes in those routines will cause distress. Some pupils with Autistic Spectrum Disorders have a different perception of sounds, sights, smell, touch and taste, and this can affect their response to these sensations.

How can the art teacher help?

- Liaise with parents as they will have many useful strategies.

- Make full use of all visual supports in class: objects, artist reproductions, other pupils' work etc.

- Give a symbolic, coloured or written timetable for each day.

- Give advance warning of any changes to usual routines, e.g. when progressing from sketchbook work into the practicalities of 3D work.

- Provide either an individual desk or with a work buddy.

- Avoid using too much eye contact as it can cause distress.

- Give individual instructions using the pupil's name, e.g. 'Paul, bring me your sketchbook.'

- Allow access to departmental computers if possible.

- Develop social interactions using a buddy system or Circle of Friends for activities such as discussing their own or artists' work.

- Avoid using metaphor, idiom or sarcasm – say what you mean in simple language.

- Use special interests to motivate, e.g. by allowing a pupil to develop their own painting project.

- Allow difficult situations to be rehearsed by means of social stories based on artworks that provoke thought or prompt discussion that could be led by another pupil.

BEHAVIOURAL, EMOTIONAL AND SOCIAL DEVELOPMENT NEEDS

This term includes behavioural, emotional and social difficulties and Attention Deficit Disorder with or without hyperactivity. These difficulties can be seen across the whole ability range and have a continuum of severity. Pupils with special educational needs in this category are those who have persistent difficulties despite an effective school behaviour policy and a personal and social curriculum.

Behavioural, emotional, social difficulties (BESD)

Main characteristics

- inattentive, poor concentration and lacks interest in school/school work
- easily frustrated, anxious about changes
- unable to work in groups
- unable to work independently, constantly seeking help
- confrontational – verbally aggressive towards pupils and/or adults
- physically aggressive towards pupils and/or adults
- destroys property – their own/others'
- appears withdrawn, distressed, unhappy, sulky, may self-harm
- lacks confidence, acts extremely frightened, lacks self-esteem
- finds it difficult to communicate
- finds it difficult to accept praise

How can the art teacher help?

- Check the ability level of the pupil and adapt the level of work to this.
- Consider the pupil's strengths and use them.
- Tell the pupil what you expect in advance, for work and behaviour.
- Talk to the pupil to find out a bit about them. You could ask them to draw about this in their class or homework.
- Set art skill-based targets with a reward system, e.g. improving shading techniques by . . .
- Focus your comments on the behaviour not on the pupil and offer an alternative way of behaving when correcting the pupil.

- Use positive language and verbal praise whenever possible.

- Tell the pupil what you want them to do: 'I need you to . . .', 'I want you to . . .' rather than ask. This avoids confrontation and the possibility that there is room for negotiation.

- Give the pupil a choice between two options. For example, when using materials, 'Would you like to use oil pastels or watercolours?'

- Stick to what you say.

- Involve the pupil in responsibilities to increase self-esteem and confidence.

- Plan a 'time out' system. Ask a colleague for help with this.

Association of Workers for Children with Emotional and Behavioural Difficulties
Website: www.awcebd.co.uk

Cerebral palsy (CP)

Cerebral palsy is a persistent disorder of movement and posture. It is caused by damage or lack of development to part of the brain before or during birth or in early childhood. Problems vary from slight clumsiness to more severe lack of control of movements. Pupils with CP may also have learning difficulties. They may use a wheelchair or other mobility aid.

Main characteristics

There are three main forms of cerebral palsy:

- **spasticity** – disordered control of movement associated with stiffened muscles

- **athetosis** – frequent involuntary movements

- **ataxia** – an unsteady gait with balance difficulties and poor spatial awareness

Pupils may also have communication difficulties.

How can the art teacher help?

- Talk to parents, the physiotherapist – and the pupil.

- Consider the classroom layout.

- Have high expectations.

- Use a wide variety of visual supports: objects/artefacts, pictures, symbols, colour.

- Arrange a work/subject buddy.

- Speak directly to the pupil rather than through a teaching assistant.

- Ensure access to appropriate IT equipment for the subject in class if possible, via a computer or laptop – and make sure that it is used.

Scope, PO BOX 833, Milton Keynes, MK12 5NY
Tel: 0808 800 3333 (Freephone helpline) Fax: 01908 321051
Email: cphelpline@scope.org.uk Website: http://www.scope.org.uk

Down's Syndrome (DS)

Down's Syndrome is the most common identifiable cause of learning disability. This is a genetic condition caused by the presence of an extra chromosome 21. People with DS have varying degrees of learning difficulties ranging from mild to severe. They have a specific learning profile with characteristic strengths and weaknesses. All share certain physical characteristics but will also inherit family traits in physical features and personality. They may have additional sight, hearing, respiratory and heart problems.

Main characteristics

- delayed motor skills
- take longer to learn and consolidate new skills
- limited concentration
- difficulties with generalisation, thinking and reasoning
- sequencing difficulties
- stronger visual than aural skills
- better social than academic skills

How can the art teacher help?

- Ensure that the pupil is able to see and hear you and other pupils.
- Speak directly to the pupil and reinforce with facial expression, pictures and objects.
- Use simple, familiar language in short sentences.
- Check instructions have been understood.
- Give time to process information and formulate a response, either verbally or via artwork.
- Break lessons up into a series of shorter, varied and achievable tasks.
- Accept a variety of ways of recording: drawings, tape/video recordings, collage, etc.
- Set differentiated tasks linked to the work of the rest of the class.
- Provide age-appropriate resources and activities.
- Allow working in top sets to give good behaviour models.
- Provide a work buddy.
- Expect unsupported work for part of each lesson.

Downs' Syndrome Association, Langdon Down Centre, 2a Langdon Park, Teddington TW11 9PS
Tel: 0845 230 0372 Fax: 0845 230 0373
Email: info@downs-syndrome.org.uk Website: http://www.downs-syndrome.org.uk

Fragile X Syndrome

Fragile X Syndrome is caused by a malformation of the X chromosome and is the most common form of inherited learning disability. This intellectual disability varies widely, with up to a third having learning problems ranging from moderate to severe. More boys than girls are affected but both may be carriers.

Main characteristics

- delayed and disordered speech and language development
- difficulties with the social use of language
- articulation and/or fluency difficulties
- verbal skills better developed than reasoning skills
- repetitive or obsessive behaviour, such as hand-flapping, chewing etc.
- clumsiness and fine motor co-ordination problems
- attention deficit and hyperactivity
- easily anxious or overwhelmed in busy environments

How can the art teacher help?

- Liaise with parents.
- Make sure the pupil knows what is to happen in each lesson – provide visual timetables, work schedules or written lists – or set routines.
- Ensure the pupil sits near teacher, in the same seat for all lessons.
- Arrange a work/subject buddy.
- Where possible keep to routines and give prior warning of all changes.
- Make instructions clear and simple.
- Use a variety of visual supports: objects/artefacts, pictures, symbols, colour.
- Allow the pupil to use a computer (better still, a laptop) to record and access information, e.g. when researching/looking at the work of an artist.
- Give lots of praise and positive feedback, especially focusing on art skills such as use of colour, texture, tone etc.

Fragile X Society, Rood End House, 6 Stortford Road, Dunmow CM6 1DA
Tel: 01424 813147 (Helpline) Tel: 01371 875100 (Office)
Email: info@fragilex.org.uk Website: http://www.fragilex.org.uk

Moderate learning difficulties (MLD)

This term is used to describe pupils who find it extremely difficult to achieve expected levels of attainment across the curriculum, even with a differentiated and flexible approach. These pupils do not find learning easy and can suffer from low self-esteem and sometimes exhibit unacceptable behaviour as a way of avoiding failure.

Main characteristics

- difficulties with reading, writing and comprehension
- unable to understand and retain basic mathematical skills and concepts
- immature social and emotional skills
- limited vocabulary and communication skills
- short attention span
- underdeveloped co-ordination skills
- lack of logical reasoning
- inability to transfer and apply skills to different situations
- difficulty remembering what has been taught
- difficulty with organising themselves, following a timetable, remembering books and equipment

How can the art teacher help?

- Check the pupil's strengths, weaknesses and attainment levels.
- Establish a routine within the lesson.
- Keep tasks short and varied.
- Keep listening tasks short, highlighting the main points only.
- Provide word lists or display key words/formal elements in imaginative ways, such as a mobile. Read aloud minimum background information on an artist/movement/genre, supplying relative descriptive words, skills, art-specific language via a list or display, (e.g. examples of use of texture etc.).
- Try alternative methods of recording information, e.g. drawings, labelling, use of ICT.
- Check previously gained knowledge and build on this.
- Repeat information in different ways.
- Show the child what to do or what the expected outcome is, demonstrate or show examples of completed work.
- Use practical, concrete, visual examples to illustrate explanations.
- Question the pupil to check they have grasped a concept or can follow instructions.
- Make sure the pupil always has something to do.
- Use lots of praise, instant rewards – catch them trying hard.

The MLD Alliance, c/o The Elfrida Society, 34 Islington Park Street, London N1 1PX
www.mldalliance.com/excutive.htm

Physical disability (PD)

There is a wide range of physical disabilities, and pupils with PD cover all academic abilities. Some pupils are able to access the curriculum and learn effectively without additional educational provision. They have a disability but do not have a special educational need. For other pupils, the impact on their education may be severe and the school will need to make adjustments to enable them to access the curriculum.

Some pupils with a physical disability have associated medical conditions which may impact on their mobility. These include cerebral palsy, heart disease, spina bifida, hydrocephalus and muscular dystrophy. Pupils with physical disabilities may also have sensory impairments, neurological problems or learning difficulties. They may use a wheelchair and/or additional mobility aids. Some pupils will be mobile but may have significant fine motor difficulties which require support. Others may need augmentative or alternative communication aids.

Pupils with a physical disability may need to miss lessons to attend physiotherapy or medical appointments. They are also likely to become very tired as they expend greater effort to complete everyday tasks. Schools will need to be flexible and sensitive to individual pupil needs.

How can the art teacher help?

- Get to know pupils and parents and they will help you make the right adjustments.

- Maintain high expectations.

- Consider the classroom layout.

- Allow the pupil to leave lessons a few minutes early to avoid busy corridors and give them time to get to the next lesson.

- When planning a trip or visit, liaise with the gallery or museum to assess facilities and access.

- Set homework earlier in the lesson so instructions are not missed.

- Speak directly to the pupil rather than through a teaching assistant.

- Let pupils make their own decisions, especially on how to develop a topic.

- Ensure access to appropriate IT equipment for the lesson.

- Give alternative ways of recording work, especially homework.

- Plan to cover work missed through medical or physiotherapy appointments.

- Be sensitive to fatigue, especially at the end of the school day.

Semantic Pragmatic Disorder (SPD)

Semantic Pragmatic Disorder is a communication disorder which falls within the autistic spectrum. 'Semantic' refers to the meanings of words and phrases and 'pragmatic' refers to the use of language in a social context. Pupils with this disorder have difficulties understanding the meaning of what people say and in using language to communicate effectively. Pupils with SPD find it difficult to extract the central meaning – saliency – of situations.

Main characteristics

- delayed language development

- fluent speech but may sound stilted or over-formal

- may repeat phrases out of context from videos or adult conversations

- difficulty understanding abstract concepts

- limited or inappropriate use of eye contact, facial expression or gesture

- motor skills problems

How can the art teacher help?

- Sit the pupil near to the teacher to avoid distractions.

- Use a variety of visual supports: objects/artefacts, pictures, symbols, colour etc.

- Pair with a work/subject buddy.

- Create a calm working environment with clear classroom rules.

- Be specific and unambiguous when giving instructions.

- Make sure instructions are understood, especially when using subject-specific vocabulary that can have another meaning in a different context. Whenever possible, display examples of subject vocabulary around the room with relative images or colours etc.

AFASIC, 2nd Floor, 50–52 Great Sutton Street, London EC1V 0DJ
Tel: 0845 355 5577 (Helpline) Tel: 020 7490 9410 Fax: 020 7251 2834
Email: info@afasic.org.uk Website: http://www.afasic.org.uk

Sensory impairments

Hearing impairment (HI)

The term 'hearing impairment' is a generic term used to describe all hearing loss. The main types of loss are monaural, conductive, sensory and mixed loss. The degree of hearing loss is described as mild, moderate, severe or profound.

How can the art teacher help?

- Check the degree of hearing loss the pupil has.

- Check the best seating position (e.g. away from the hum of computers, with good ear to speaker).

- Check that the pupil can see your face for facial expressions and lip reading.

- Provide a list of subject-specific terms/vocabulary, context and visual stimuli, especially for new topics.

- During group discussion allow one pupil to speak at a time and indicate where the speaker is.

- Check that any aids are working and whether there is any other specialist equipment available.

Royal Institute for the Deaf (RNID), 19–23 Featherstone Street, London EC1Y 8SL
Tel: 0808 808 0123
British Deaf Association (BDA), 1–3 Worship Street, London EC2A 2AB
British Association of Teachers of the Deaf (BATOD), The Orchard, Leven, North Humberside HU17 5QA Website: www.batod.org.uk

Visual impairment (VI)

'Visual impairment' refers to a range of difficulties including those pupils with monocular vision (vision in one eye), those who are partially sighted and those who are blind. Pupils with visual impairment cover the whole ability range and some pupils may have other SEN.

How can the art teacher help?

- check the optimum position for the pupil, e.g. for a monocular pupil their good eye should be towards the action.

- Always provide the pupil with his or her own copy of any text, e.g. background information on an art movement.

- Provide enlarged print copies of written text.

- Check use of ICT (enlarged icons, talking text, teach keyboard skills) and emphasise creative aspects of easy-to-use art software.

- Do not stand with your back to the window as this creates a silhouette and makes it harder for the pupil to see you.

- Draw the pupil's attention to specific displays/examples of other pupils' work – which they may not notice amongst all the other artwork on display.

- Make sure the floor is kept free of clutter and that materials, if spilt or dropped, are cleaned up immediately.

- Tell the pupil if there is a change to the layout of a space.

- Ask if there is any specialist equipment available (lights, laptops, magnifiers etc.).

Royal National Institute for the Blind, 105 Judd Street, London WC1H 9NE
Tel: 020 7388 1266 Fax: 020 7388 2034 Website: http://www.rnib.org.uk

Multi-sensory impairment

Pupils with multi-sensory impairment have a combination of visual and hearing difficulties. They may also have other additional disabilities that make their situation complex. A pupil with these difficulties is likely to have a high level of individual support.

How can the art teacher help?

- The teacher will need to liaise with support staff to ascertain the appropriate provision within each aspect of the subject.

- Consideration will need to be given to alternative means of communication.

- Be prepared to be flexible and to adapt tasks, targets and assessment procedures.

Severe learning difficulties (SLD)

This term covers a wide and varied group of pupils who have significant intellectual or cognitive impairments. Many have communication difficulties and/or sensory impairments in addition to more general cognitive impairments. They may also have difficulties in mobility, co-ordination and perception. Some pupils may use signs and symbols to support their communication and understanding. Their attainments may be within or below level 1 of the National Curriculum, or in the upper P-scale range (P4–P8), for much of their school careers.

How can the art teacher help?

- Liaise with parents.

- Arrange a work/subject buddy.

- Use a wide variety of visual supports: objects, pictures, symbols, use of colour.

- Build in opportunities within planning, to explore a multi-sensory approach.

- Learn some signs relevant to the subject.

- Allow the pupil time to process information and formulate responses.

- Set differentiated tasks linked to the work of the rest of the class.

- Set achievable targets for each lesson or module of work.

- Accept different recording methods: drawings, audio or video recordings, photographs etc.

- Give access to computers where appropriate.

- Give a series of short, varied activities within each lesson.

Profound and multiple learning difficulties (PMLD)

Pupils with profound and multiple learning difficulties have complex learning needs. In addition to very severe learning difficulties, pupils have other significant difficulties, such as physical disabilities, sensory impairments or severe medical conditions. Pupils with PMLD require a high level of adult support, both for their learning needs and for their personal care.

They are able to access the curriculum through sensory experiences and stimulation. Some pupils communicate by gesture, eye pointing or symbols, others by very simple language. Their attainments are likely to remain in the early P-scale range (P1–P4) throughout their school careers (that is below level 1 of the National Curriculum). The P-scales provide small, achievable steps to monitor progress. Some pupils will make no progress or may even regress because of associated medical conditions. For this group, experiences are as important as attainment.

How can the art teacher help?

- Liaise with parents and teaching assistants.

- Consider the classroom layout.

- Identify and plan for as many sensory experiences as possible in your lessons.

- Use additional sensory supports: objects, pictures, fragrances, music, movements, food etc.

- Take photographs to record experiences and responses.

- Set up a work/subject buddy rota for the class.

- Identify times when the pupil can work with groups, e.g. on larger-scale work or when creating a 3D piece.

MENCAP, 117–123 Golden Lane, London EC1Y 0RT
Tel: 020 7454 0454 Website: http://www.mencap.org.uk

SPECIFIC LEARNING DIFFICULTIES (SpLD)

The term 'specific learning difficulties' covers dyslexia, dyscalculia and dyspraxia.

Dyslexia

The term 'dyslexia' is used to describe a learning difficulty associated with words and it can affect a pupil's ability to read, write and/or spell. Research has shown that there is no one definitive definition of dyslexia nor one identified cause, and it has a wide range of symptoms. Although found across a whole range of ability levels, the idea that dyslexia presents as a difficulty between expected outcomes and performance is widely held.

Main characteristics

- The pupil may frequently lose their place while reading, make a lot of errors with the high frequency words, have difficulty reading names, blending sounds and segmenting words. Reading requires a great deal of effort and concentration.

- The pupil's written work may seem messy with crossing outs, similarly shaped letters may be confused, such as b/d/p/q, m/w, n/u, and letters in words may be jumbled, such as tired/tried. Spelling difficulties often persist into adult life and these pupils become reluctant writers.

How can the art teacher help?

- Be aware of the type of difficulty and the pupil's strengths.

- Teach and allow the use of word processing, spell checkers and computer-aided learning packages if needed in lessons, but especially for homework, e.g. when conducting research on an artist.

- Provide word lists and photocopies of important information linked to the topic.

- Use a variety of recording methods, e.g. collage, photographs, drawings/paintings, mind maps on a topic area that need limited writing.

- Allow extra time for tasks including assessments and examinations, e.g. when annotating sketchbook work.

The British Dyslexia Association
Tel: 0118 966 8271 Website: www.bda-dyslexia.org.uk
Dyslexia Institute
Tel: 07184 222 300 Website: www.dyslexia-inst.org.uk

Dyscalculia

The term 'dyscalculia' is used to describe a difficulty in mathematics. This might be either a marked discrepancy between the pupil's developmental level and general ability on measures of specific maths ability or a total inability to abstract or consider concepts and numbers.

Main characteristics

- *In number*, the pupil may have difficulty counting by rote, writing or reading numbers, miss out or reverse numbers, have difficulty with mental maths, and be unable to remember concepts, rules and formulae.

- *In maths* based concepts, the pupil may have difficulty with money, telling the time, with directions, right and left, with sequencing events or losing track of turns, e.g. in team games, dance.

How can the art teacher help?

- Provide help with aspects of design, 3D or composition that may need measurements to be accurate.

- If teaching perspective, use artists' work as examples rather than trying to teach it mathematically, i.e. vanishing point accuracy.

- Make use of ICT if appropriate.

- Encourage the use of sketchbooks as a means of planning and preparation.

- Allow extra time for tasks including assessments and examinations, when required.

Website: www.dyscalculia.co.uk

Dyspraxia

The term 'dyspraxia' is used to describe an immaturity with the way in which the brain processes information, resulting in messages not being properly transmitted.

Main characteristics

- difficulty in co-ordinating movements, may appear awkward and clumsy;

- difficulty with handwriting and drawing, throwing and catching;

- difficulty following sequential events, e.g. multiple instructions;

- may misinterpret situations, take things literally;

- limited social skills which result in frustration and irritability;

- some articulation difficulties (verbal dyspraxia).

How can the art teacher help?

- Be sensitive to the pupil's limitations in group activities and plan tasks to enable success.

- Ask the pupil questions to check his/her understanding of instructions/tasks.

- Check seating position to encourage good presentation (both feet resting on the floor, desk at elbow height and with ideally a sloping surface to work on).

Website: www.dyspraxiafoundation.org.uk

Speech, language and communication difficulties (SLCD)

Pupils with speech, language and communication difficulties have problems understanding what others say and/or making others understand what they say. Their development of speech and language skills may be significantly delayed. Speech and language difficulties are common in young children but most problems are resolved during the primary years. Problems that persist beyond the transfer to secondary school will be more severe. Any problem affecting speech, language and communication will have a significant effect on a pupil's self-esteem, and personal and social relationships. The development of literacy skills is also likely to be affected. Even where pupils learn to decode, they may not understand what they have read. Sign language gives pupils an additional method of communication. Pupils with speech, language and communication difficulties cover the whole range of academic abilities.

Main characteristics

- **Speech difficulties**
  Pupils who have difficulties with expressive language may experience problems in articulation and the production of speech sounds, or in co-ordinating the muscles that control speech. They may have a stammer or some other form of dysfluency.

- **Language/communication difficulties**
  Pupils with receptive language impairments have difficulty understanding the meaning of what others say. They may use words incorrectly with inappropriate grammatical patterns, have a reduced vocabulary, or find it hard to recall words and express ideas. Some pupils will also have difficulty using and understanding eye contact, facial expression, gesture and body language.

How can the art teacher help?

- Talk to parents, speech therapist – and the pupil.
- Learn the most common signs for your subject.
- Use a wide variety of visual supports: objects/artefacts, pictures, symbols, colours.
- Use the pupil's name when addressing them.
- Give one instruction at a time, using short, simple sentences.
- Give time to respond before repeating a question.
- Make sure pupils understand what they have to do before starting a task.
- Pair with a work/subject buddy.
- Give access to a computer or other IT equipment appropriate to the topic.
- Give written homework instructions.

ICAN, 4 Dyer's Buildings, Holborn, London EC1N 2QP
Tel: 0845 225 4071
Email: info@ican.org.uk Website: http://www.ican.org.uk
AFASIC 2nd Floor, 50–52 Great Sutton Street, London EC1V 0DJ
Tel: 0845 355 5577 (Helpline) Tel: 020 7490 9410 Fax: 020 7251 2834
Email: info@afasic.org.uk Website: http://www.afasic.org.uk

Tourette's Syndrome (TS)

Tourette's Syndrome is a neurological disorder characterised by tics. Tics are involuntary rapid or sudden movements or sounds that are frequently repeated. There is a wide range of severity of the condition with some people having no need to seek medical help while others have a socially disabling condition. The tics can be suppressed for a short time but will be more noticeable when the pupil is anxious or excited.

Main characteristics

- **Physical tics**
  These range from simple blinking or nodding through more complex movements to more extreme conditions such as echopraxia (imitating actions seen) or copropraxia (repeatedly making obscene gestures).

- **Vocal tics**
  Vocal tics may be as simple as throat clearing or coughing but can progress to be as extreme as echolalia (the repetition of what was last heard) or coprolalia (the repetition of obscene words).

TS itself causes no behavioural or educational problems but other, associated disorders such as Attention Deficit Hyperactivity Disorder (ADHD) or Obsessive Compulsive Disorder (OCD) may be present.

How can the art teacher help?

- Establish a rapport with the pupil.

- Talk to the parents.

- Agree an 'escape route' signal should the tics become disruptive.

- Allow the pupil to sit behind other pupils as far as possible to prevent staring.

- Agree to brief annotations and/or drawings to reduce handwriting in lesson time.

- Make sure pupil is not teased or bullied by monitoring pair/group work or small group discussions.

- Be alert for signs of anxiety or depression.

Tourette Syndrome (UK) Association
PO Box 26149, Dunfermline KY12 7YU
Tel: 0845 458 1252 (Helpline) Tel: 01383 629600 (Admin) Fax: 01383 629609
Email: enquiries@tsa.org.uk Website: http://www.tsa.org.uk

What Can Art and Design Offer Pupils with SEN?

Art is not everything but to miss out on it is to deprive us of a whole world of values brought to the senses. (Louis Arnaud Reid)

Art and design is a fundamental and unique form of experience which cannot be replicated. David Hockney states:

I do believe that art should be a deep pleasure and part of everyone's life. I do not think we can live without art of some form. (*The Guardian*, 10 November 1995)

The NCC Arts in Schools Project Team in 1989 stated that:

the value of art, craft and design education for pupils with SEN is not to compensate for abilities that children and young people don't have, but to identify and develop the abilities they do have.

Central to art and design lies the development of the senses based on observation, imagination and memory. Sight, touch, feeling and intellect need to be developed through an understanding of the elements of visual language, for example, line, colour, texture, shape, form and space.

Direct handling and manipulation of materials and the development of skills build upon a child's natural interest and pleasure in rhythm, movement, shape and colour. For the SEN pupil, as with all pupils, personal experience and personal responses may be a starting point for an art activity. In order for children to gain skills and confidence in themselves as artists and designers, there must be a degree of success in all activities.

In designing an art and design course the following aims are an integral part of the planning, bearing in mind that the expectations of process and outcome

are commensurate with the child's level of development and ability. The equipment and materials provided also must match the motor control and manual dexterity of the pupil involved.

Aims are to:

- Develop an understanding, appreciation and enjoyment of art and design, where possible, in historical, functional and aesthetic terms.

- Develop a sense of enquiry about visual and tactile experiences.

- Enable pupils to realise their creative intentions, through the development of technical competence and manipulative skills.

- Be aware of the social and cultural context within which a pupil lives and works.

- Provide opportunities for personal and imaginative enquiry; it is essential that pupils with special needs are given many opportunities for creative expression and the use of hand-eye co-ordination.

- Observe, record, evaluate and order information.

- Encourage pupils to be self-critical and self-motivated and to develop the ability to solve problems.

- Help pupils acquire a subject-specific language.

- Encourage experimentation and help develop a means of personal expression.

- Have fun and enjoyment and feel stimulated by the sense of achievement in the creative process.

An essential element in art and design teaching is a degree of 'uncertainty', a chance for pupils to discover the potential of materials and processes within a carefully 'safe' and structured environment.

A range of opportunities commensurate with the needs and abilities should be on offer to all pupils and appropriate provision should be made for those pupils who need emphasis placed on the tactile approach to art and design. Appropriate provision should be made for pupils who need:

- non-sighted methods such as braille, non-visual or non-aural methods of acquiring information;

- means of communication other than speech, including appropriate ICT equipment, signing, symbols and lip reading;

- technological aids in practical and written work;

- aids and adapted equipment to allow access to practical activities within school and in museums/galleries and site visits.

When planning for SEN pupils, material may be selected from earlier or later key stages to enable progress and demonstrate achievement, but all material should be presented in contexts suitable to the pupil's age. Teachers need to clarify the minimum requirement and the potential development of the 'art' task in hand and to ensure that pupils understand what is expected of them.

Clear instructions and demonstrations (often one to one) as well as ongoing supervision are vital in a practical classroom, with adequate time allowed for a lead in to creative work and a time to tidy up at the end of the activity.

In order to develop visual literacy *all* pupils should be taught about different ways in which ideas, feelings and meanings are communicated in visual form. Disabilities should never become the basis for limitation of experience.

All children should be given a forum and challenge for discussing and making sense of their experiences and understanding in the arts. Above all, art and design may help pupils to develop as discerning adults, able to make informed judgements, developing confidence and their own sense of worth.

An inclusive environment

There is a lot that can be done in terms of the physical environment to make activities more accessible and safe for pupils with special needs. Tables that can be adjusted for height (and slope), chairs, stools and easels of different heights are expensive items but can be bought over time to broaden the range of furniture in the art room. Remember to leave adequate space around furniture for pupils to be able to move around easily (including any wheelchair users) and keep the floor clear of bags and coats. A quiet corner, partly screened from the rest of the room and 'quietly' decorated, can be a useful resource for pupils who sometimes need 'time out' – for whatever reason.

Store equipment and materials in clearly labelled boxes/drawers/cupboards within reach of all pupils and with labels big enough to be read by those with less than perfect eyesight. Pupils with visual impairment benefit from a static room layout – getting to know where the obstacles are and how to move safely around them; but where this is not possible, ask another pupil to help out with the reorientation process. Braille can be employed where appropriate.

It is important to display examples of best practice and to show pupils work and subject-specific language. It may be appropriate to display an artefact or painting weekly or monthly and refer to this as 'Painting of the Month', for example. Simple display is often the key to success. It is important to encourage the process to be exhibited alongside the finished piece: photographs of pupils working, the plan of work, artefacts which extend the work, and appropriate and clearly written statements. Displays on the walls can be inaccessible to some pupils with visual impairment and to wheelchair users if the display is positioned too high up – important considerations to take into account.

In order to be able to offer pupils a variety of opportunities in art and design, a pool of resources and materials has to be available. Quality materials and quality display support quality work and set a high standard for pupils to emulate. A selection of videos, slides, interactive ICT programmes, digital cameras, posters, books, artefacts (on loan from museums or the LEA etc.) and teacher/gallery education packs should be available in the art department. The support of other professional experts, such as advisory staff, is another resource to enhance provision.

Safety tips

Safety tips relating to specific projects should be displayed around the room and attention drawn to them verbally and visually at the beginning of each lesson. Some pupils with SEN may require continued support from a teaching or classroom assistant throughout.

- Round-nosed and a choice of right and left-handed scissors should be available in the artroom.

- Glue used should be a washable PVA where necessary or a low-temperature electric glue gun.

- PVA is a suitable substitute for varnish. If varnish is used, supervision is necessary.

- Incising polystyrene may be done with biros rather than sharp tools.

- Printing inks should be non-toxic and water-based.

- Care must be taken with the handling of mirrors – reflective plastic tiles are a suitable alternative.

- Water-soluble non-toxic inks and paints must be an alternative within the artroom.

- Sharp metallic objects or chicken wire may require gloves and goggles to be worn.

- Great care should be taken when using hot wax (batik) – ensure all flexes are taped down to avoid accidents and that pupils are supervised at all times, including when handling dyes.

- There should be supervision of the cutting of doweling. The wearing of goggles may be appropriate when handling willow or canes.

Differentiation

Art and design education provides practical learning experiences which are accessible to pupils of all abilities. Using appropriate and differentiated work is about making tasks accessible to the whole range of pupils within a class or teaching group. In the art department a variety of methods should be used rather than a reliance on one or two and differentiation also needs to pay cognisance to pupils' preferred ways of learning. Multi-sensory approaches are vital in the art classroom.

In Chapter 5 the range of projects discussed gives a variety of starting points, material usage, skill acquisition and support techniques. The following definitions may help clarify the variety of possibilities in planning for art projects for pupils with SEN.

Differentiation by outcome

The same material or stimulus is used for all pupils or the same tasks are set for everybody in the group. Differentiation is achieved by individuals answering at their own levels of ability, so that different outcomes form the same task or piece of work. For example, in the Iron Man project (Chapter 5) the starting point is the popular children's book *The Iron Man* by Ted Hughes. This may be developed into 3D, print, painting or assemblage according to the individual's needs and abilities.

Differentiation by resource

This method is based on the fact that some pupils are capable of working with more advanced techniques than others. They may be responding to the same basic starting point but have more in-depth skill acquisition; for example, print making can involve sequential processes that may require specialist tools and equipment, or it can involve simple mono printing techniques to fulfil the task. The Water project in Chapter 5 could be extended to include these techniques, using a variety of materials such as lino and woodblock.

Differentiation by task

A variety of tasks are provided that cover the main content area so as to provide for the range of individual pupils in the group or class. Homework as well as lesson work is effective when differentiated to the needs of the pupils. For example, when researching the Forms in the Landscape project (Chapter 5) for homework, pupils could be set different tasks as starting points such as collecting natural forms, sketching views from their local landscape, finding information on the Internet and fact-finding on a landscape artist.

Differentiation by dialogue

The vocabulary and complexity of language needs to vary for different pupils. In order to develop visual literacy pupils should be taught about different ways in which ideas, feelings and meanings are communicated in visual and linguistic forms. The skilled teacher will introduce the pupil to an 'art' vocabulary and prompt and encourage the pupil by comments suitable to their ability and the degree of progress being made. For example, when looking at a Picasso portrait, the teacher may prepare prompt cards prior to the lessons that will allow pupils to explore the formal art elements.

Differentiation by support

The amount and degree of practical and other help provided should be differentiated to meet the needs of individual pupils. The teacher, support staff, other pupils and appropriate ICT or other hardware may give extra support to the pupil with SEN in the art room. For example, a pupil with poor motor skills may be able to respond to a task using a laptop and modified mouse and Photoshop software that will allow him/her to modify and adapt a series of self-portraits or photographs taken on a digital camera, such as changing colour and distortion.

Differentiation by pace

Some pupils need to move forward more gradually than others; some pupils may become confused if tasks and concepts are presented too rapidly. Incremental, step-by-step approaches help the development and consolidation of concepts and skills. Art lesson planning can be differentiated in terms of how much and how quickly tasks are to be completed. In art and design it is important to allow time for analysis, reflection and discussion and include a period for experimentation to discover the potential of materials and processes.

Differentiation by pupil grouping

The organisation of pupils into working groups at a class level is a feature of differentiation. Consideration needs to be given to this in order to respond to changing needs and to pupils' differing abilities in a wide range of art materials and related skills. The teacher should ensure that the group dynamics and relationships provide a supportive environment for each pupil to contribute to the final piece, as with the Man and Machine Project in Chapter 6.

Differentiation by responsibility

Allow pupils to take some responsibility for their learning. The teacher may provide them with open-ended tasks and projects where the pupils make decisions about skill development, for example a drawing developing into print or textiles.

Differentiation in planning

As well as ensuring the effective delivery of art and design, schemes of work should demonstrate differentiation of approach similar to those mentioned above. The 'Must, Should, Could' model as highlighted in the National Curriculum guidance aims to ensure that pupils of all abilities achieve in lessons.

Planning within art and design

Effective planning takes account of the different abilities and interests of each pupil, allowing them to progress and demonstrate their achievements. A balanced programme of study is one which develops skills in painting, drawing, collage, 3D work, printing and textiles alongside an understanding of colour, line, texture, pattern, shape, form and space.

When planning a unit of work, the following points need to be included:

- title of unit of work or project;
- skills highlighted, e.g. drawing, painting, printing, 3D, textiles collage;
- elements highlighted, e.g. pattern, colour, line, shape, tone, form and space;
- learning objectives;
- teacher input and other staff support;
- investigating and making;
- knowledge and understanding;
- assessment opportunities;
- resources including gallery visits etc.;
- skills highlighted within the unit of work;
- health and safety considerations.

Within the long-term and medium-term planning, the following checklist needs to be considered with pupils with SEN in mind:

- List the learning difficulties of pupils within the class or group.
- Indicate any Statemented pupils and the nature of their special provision, including health and safety implications and medical procedures.

- Outline any support teacher time available.

- Outline responsibilities of the support teacher.

- List any learning support resources available.

- Indicate any targeted funding for SEN support for art.

- List special provision needed for examinations and assessment, also indicating methods of recording progress for pupils with SEN when necessarily different from the rest of the pupils.

- Indicate time when pupils may have 'tutorials' or individual assessments.

  My sculpture can last for days or for a few seconds – what is important for me is the experience of making. (Andy Goldsworthy)

Progression statements in the skills and elements of each project are important and work should be built upon over a period of time, rather than a series of 'one-off' lessons.

Many skills and elements will be repeated, such as the skill of drawing, the elements of line and colour, and in a pupil's IEP it is important to stress progression in the development of skills and the understanding of the formal elements of art and design. (See example IEP, p. 127)

A folder for each child, including their sketchpad, digital photographs of their work, records of visits, work with artists etc., helps a pupil to take a pride in their artwork and achievements. It is not necessary for every piece of work to be related to the work of an artist. However, art education and pupils' practice may be closely linked with how artists work, the materials they use, the thinking and working processes involved and their specialist vocabulary.

Links with artists

Links with artists are important either at a gallery or as part of an Artist-in-Residency scheme. The objectives of such a scheme are to introduce pupils to the concept of an artist as a professional 'working' person, to experience the creative process and to have the opportunity to work and exhibit alongside an artist. Working with an artist can enable teachers to learn new skills, to refresh their own knowledge and understanding of the arts. It may also give the teacher an opportunity to stand back and observe their pupils in a new situation, developing confidence, thus gaining a new insight into their pupils' achievement and potential.

A publication *From Policy to Partnership*, published jointly by QCA and the Arts Council of England (QCA/ACE 2000) and distributed with Curriculum 2000, highlights the advantages of arts partnerships:

> Partnerships can offer pupils a much greater range and depth of arts experiences than can be provided by school alone.

The energy and enthusiasm engendered by such collaborations, for example between industry, school, teachers, artists, pupils and the community, genuinely enhance the learning and enjoyment of art.

It is necessary to use a range of artists, craftspeople and designers to enable pupils to develop an appreciation of our rich and diverse cultural heritage. A variety of styles from the locality, historical and contemporary, and from both Western and non-Western cultures should be selected.

Using ICT in art and design

In Key Stage 3, pupils will be developing their creativity and skills in a range of materials and processes – including ICT. The use of ICT equipment and software can do a lot to maximise opportunities for pupils, particularly for those with SEN. Problems of fine motor control can be addressed; images can be enlarged to help overcome visual impairment; (predictive) word processing can be a boon to those with poor literacy/handwriting skills. The use of digital photography has revolutionised classroom practice, as illustrated by the project outlined on pp. 52–3.

Products like the Art Pad allow pupils to control graphics applications with a pressure-sensitive pen rather than a conventional mouse, and experiment with a wide range of effects. (See Resources). A wide range of software and websites is evaluated by *Evaluate* and *Schoolzone* in association with the DfES (www.learnevaluations.co.uk;www.schoolzone.co.uk).

AN EXAMPLE OF AN ART PROJECT WITH SPECIAL SCHOOLS

Digital artwork led by artist Dorrie Halliday with students from across four special schools in St Helens, October 2002 for one week, at Haydock City Learning Centre.

This event was set up to celebrate national Excellence in Cities week in St Helens in October 2002. Excellence in Cities is a national strategy funded by DfES for state schools in inner-city areas. It does not support special schools and this event was a way for the Local Education Authority to offer them the opportunity to experience a high profile activity with a leading professional artist that they may not normally have had the opportunity to participate in due to lack of specific funding.

The event took place at Haydock City Learning Centre, a state-of-the-art ICT facility built for schools and the community with Excellence in Cities funding. The theme was 'The Discovery of DNA – the case for Rosalind Franklin', the story of how researchers believe that the real person who discovered DNA was female scientist Rosalind Franklin and not the two male scientists Watson and Crick. This made the project cross-curricular, looking at elements of art, science, ICT and PSHE.

Prior to the week, participating students had been identified by school staff as high achievers or potentially able in art and design. Dorrie then asked them to collect images of things associated with DNA and save them onto a CD. Students scanned in old family photographs, took digital photographs of friends, pets and themselves and brought them with them on the first day at the City Learning Centre.

The students worked over five days during half-term. There were 16 students, four from each of St Helens' special schools. They were a mixed ability group with some who had severe learning difficulties, two who were in wheelchairs, some who had very limited motor skills and a student with ADHD. All students were in Years 8 or 9. A teacher and a carer from each school supported students for all five days.

The aim of the project was for students to produce two digitally manipulated compositions on the theme of DNA. One piece was to use the images Dorrie had brought in of DNA strands, Rosalind Franklin, animals, people, the human body and so on. She had already loaded these onto the PCs in order for students to learn how to use the Photoshop software immediately. Some of Dorrie's images were original photographs; some were taken off the Internet. The other piece was to be created by the students just using their own images.

The students had no previous experience of using Photoshop but within the week they had learned:

- how to use Photoshop 6 with the support of Dorrie and her colleague – especially using masking techniques which are only available in this version of Photoshop or newer versions;
- how to use standard professional equipment and digital imaging techniques;
- to work quickly developing their own imagery – most did more than two images and one did nine! This particular student lacked fine motor skills and said that she really enjoyed working in this way as she felt she couldn't draw effectively with a pencil since she shook so much. The use of a mouse and computer made it much easier to achieve her outcomes;
- how to print images, cut and prepare them, laminate the images themselves, hook and eye with support, cut ribbons to tie work together to form a hanging from the final artwork. A separate set was prepared for the City Learning Centre's permanent display;

- how to create 'special' DNA using cardboard tubes, glitter, ribbons etc. to create their own DNA chains.

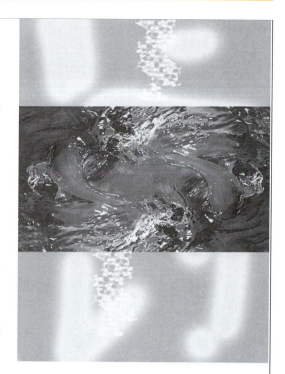

As the abilities within the group were so varied, Dorrie had to do a lot of her planning on the first day when she met the students for the first time. She worked closely with support staff to ensure they learned along with the students so that they could assist as much as needed. Each day everyone had lunch together and chatted about their work, taking time to look at what each other had done and discuss the processes and outcomes. The City Learning Centre had an excellent quality colour laser printer so that when printed out, the images looked first class.

Health and Safety

- Dorrie stopped the students at least every 45 minutes to take a break – lots of refreshments were provided! The students were so enthusiastic she had to *make* them go out and have a break!
- Dorrie advised students to look away from the computer and 'stretch' their eyes.
- The room had to be checked prior to the students' arrival to allow enough space for wheelchairs; also there were constant checks to make sure no one could trip over crutches or other personal equipment.

Dorrie led all these sessions as she would with any other students – she did not feel that their particular needs hindered them in any way. Their enthusiasm and complete enjoyment resulted in high quality images and learning processes that they will never forget. They started their own e-portfolios but also had hard copies to keep in sketchpads and mount for display in class.

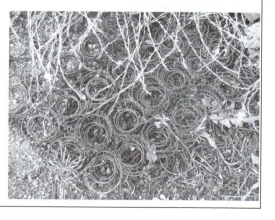

Research work

In 2002 the Standards and Effectiveness Unit of the DfES produced materials that focus specifically on Literacy in Art and Design. The following examples in this section are all taken from this strategy. The Key Stage 3 English strand developed a teaching sequence for writing and this sequence is one of its cornerstones for improving pupils' standard of writing. Art teachers may find this particularly useful as written responses can provide important evidence of a pupil's knowledge and understanding in the subject. Before use, the teachers should ensure that the purpose of doing this activity is explicit, as students do need to see the point of writing in an art lesson. Support should also be given in structuring the writing, employing the appropriate style and vocabulary. The following examples may be used with students but may equally be used with other staff in the art department as a route to planning for the inclusion of literacy. (A blank planning sheet is provided on the accompanying CD.)

Establish clear aims	Pupils will write more effectively if they understand that their writing has a real purpose.
Provide examples	Showing pupils an example of a successful outcome defines their task more precisely and gives them a model to work towards.
Explore the features of the text	The features of the example that give it quality and make it effective need to be pointed out as only the more able writers will see for themselves how the writing was done.
Define the conventions	It is useful to summarise the key features of the type of writing so that pupils know what to include.
Demonstrate how it is written	These parts of the sequence constitute an activity called 'shared writing'. Pupils should be familiar with this from primary school.
Compose together	
Scaffold the first attempts	This is a bridge between shared writing, which is teacher-led, and independent writing. Some pupils need further support to make this step to independence. This process can take place as part of the shared writing process or by the use of idea banks, word banks or writing frames.
Independent writing	This is our main goal: the previous steps are designed to give pupils the confidence to write independently and achieve a successful outcome.
Draw out key learning	It is important that pupils reflect on the outcome of their work in order to recognise progress and consolidate what has been learned.

A sequence for teaching writing (Crown copyright)

Many art teachers find the use of art journals a more effective way of promoting and consolidating learning through writing. The example below of a Year 8 piece of work could be further enhanced and made more visually appealing with the addition of Aboriginal designs, patterns and colours as a background in coloured pencil or watercolour or quite simply, with some small-scale sketches of Aboriginal designs or artefacts.

PERSPECTIVES – AUSTRALIAN ABORIGINAL ART

The theme of my work is 'Perspectives' and I have been looking at Australian Aboriginal art. All my ideas are related to this theme. The main task is to produce a lifeline in the style of Aboriginal art, but as part of the preparation I have completed some practical and written work. I have taken several artists' work into consideration and I focused on the artist Tim Leura Tjapaltjarri for my critical study. I particularly like the earthy colours and lively use of symbols in his work.

| Introduction gives clear outline of topic/ project

| Adjectives used for value judgements

During the early stages of my project I developed my understanding of how to work with symbols by working on the task of representing how I travel to school. I was able to express my inner thoughts through colour, which linked with symbols and dots, which I developed by looking at other artists' work.

| First person singular for individual explanation, reflection and evaluation

At the beginning of the project I experimented with colour and shape in an abstract way. By looking at my 'journey to school' work, I was able to gather more ideas together and strengthen my plans for my lifeline. This led me to the idea of drawing a baby's dummy to represent when I was born, but as I moved on I didn't know what other forms or shapes I could use and I became really frustrated. It was at this point that I decided to look closely at my critical study again to help me with my work. The image I looked at was called 'Napperby Death Spirit Dreaming' by Tim Leura Tjapaltjarri and is about his life story.

| Connecting phrases indicate sequence of developing work

| Subject-specific terminology used

I also completed a homework task about dreamtime where I used the Internet to find out more about what dreamtime means. I think that dreamtime is a very complicated idea, but it is also very interesting.

I was particularly interested in the way that dreamtime links with the giants and animals that came out from under the earth, and the way that was supposed to have shaped the landscape.

| Ends with a final reflective summary comment and statement of personal preferences

---

Example entry from a Year 8 art and design journal (Crown copyright)

An art journal is like a diary and includes the critical study element of your work in art. It is where you experiment, collect images and explain the thoughts and ideas you have about your own art and design work.

It can include:

- Outlines of projects

- First ideas/brainstorms on projects

- Sketches with annotations and explanations showing how your ideas develop

- Information about artists you look at and descriptions of their work

- Reproductions of the artwork you write about

- Reflections on the artwork as it progressed

- Evaluations on the strengths and weaknesses of your final pieces

Suggestions for journal entries:

SUGGESTED STRUCTURE	SENTENCE STARTERS
Introduction	*This project is about. . .* *This project we were given was. . .*
Early ideas (including visuals)	*The first thing I did was to brainstorm my ideas. . .* *A critical decision was. . .* *Talking to other people helped me think of. . .* *Looking ahead, I decided. . .*
Sources drawn on	*I started by looking up. . .* *I looked at the work of. . . and. . .* *I like the work of. . . because. . .*
Annotated reproductions (visuals)	
Information about artists	*I found out that (name of artist) had been inspired by. . .* *The time that (name) lived influenced his work because. . .*
How the work developed (including visuals)	*To start with I. . .* *Later on I. . .* *At this point I judged. . .* *I develop the work further by. . .*
Problems and difficulties (if any) and how these were overcome	*A critical moment was. . .* *When I got stuck I. . .* *As a result I decided to. . .*
Strengths and weaknesses of final piece	*I was pleased with. . .* *On reflection. . .* *I need to work harder at my. . .*

Keeping an art and design journal (Crown copyright)

HELP WITH CRITICAL STUDIES. WRITING FRAME TO USE AS A GUIDE WHEN WRITING ABOUT ARTWORK

FOCUS	PROMPTS
1. Background information Who made the image or artefact? What is it called? Where does it come from? What tradition does it belong to?	*The piece of art that I have chosen to write about is called. . .* *The artist or designer who made this piece is. . .* *He/she lives and works in. . .* *It comes from the tradition of. . .* *(e.g. European painting/Aboriginal art/Chinese ceramics. . .)*
2. What can you see? What is it made from? Is the image realistic or abstract? Describe accurately what you see.	*The piece is constructed from. . ./painted in. . ./drawn in. . .* *In the picture I can see. . .* *The sculpture looks like. . .*
3. Meaning What do you think it is about? Does it tell a story? Can you find out what the maker thought about when making this?	*The picture/sculpture/photograph makes me think of. . .* *I think the artist/photographer means to say that. . .* *It makes the viewer think of. . .*
4. How has it been made up? How have the following been used: texture, shape, form, space, line, tone and colour, composition, objects and symbols?	*Examples of sentences here:* *The artist has used line to define the edges of objects.* *By blending in all the edges, the artist has created an organic form.* *This composition is dynamic and takes your eyes in lots of different directions.* *The use of close-ups makes us feel near the character in the photograph.*
5. What materials and processes have been used? Materials: natural, made, ephemeral, precious. Processes: painting, drawing, printmaking, sculpture, digital media.	*The artist has used. . .* *This piece is made out of. . .* *Materials are used to create a powerful effect by. . .*
6. What do you think of it? What do you like about it? Why? What don't you like? Why? Why did you choose to write about it? What might you like to ask the maker? How might you take ideas to use in your own work?	*I chose to write about this piece because. . .* *What I particularly liked about this piece is. . . This is because. . .* *What works well in this piece is the. . .* *I like everything in this piece except. . .* *This is because. . .* *I have been inspired by this work to experiment with. . .* *I would like to ask the maker: why they chose. . . / what they were thinking about when. . . / who inspired them?*

A teacher's guide to assist pupils responding to a piece of artwork (Crown copyright)

The notes on keeping an art and design journal are also featured on the accompanying CD and can be adjusted for use by students directly. These provide a sound structure for recording what has been done in a project which can be completed at the end or filled in a bit at a time as the project progresses. Again, this can be made more appealing with the addition of sketches, colour, pattern, etc. and attention should be given to the extent to which the pupil with special needs can complete it. Consider enlarging the text, allowing more space for writing, using a coloured background or coloured font etc. to meet pupils' individual needs. Alternatively, think about taping or videoing the pupil's response using the sheet as a prompt only.

The key ingredients for success when teaching writing in art and design lessons are:

- Understand the individual needs of the students and adapt any written work to suit these needs.

- Utilise drawing etc. as much as possible.

- Identify a specific objective and clear purpose for the writing.

- Provide good quality, accessible examples so that pupils understand what is expected of them.

- Demonstrate the writing.

- Provide support such as writing frames for those who initially need them.

- Review success of the writing in relation to purpose.

The next steps for the Head of Department would be to:

- Compile a portfolio of successful annotated work in art, so that pupils can see and understand what is required.

- Identify a unit in a scheme of work which may benefit from some revision in light of these examples of writing approaches and use that as a starting point for development into all schemes.

Internet

Another important aspect of research is accessing the Internet. We have identified several websites at the back of this book which you will be able to access to find out relevant information on artworks, artists, craft and design. The nature of these websites varies and some may be more useful to teachers when planning work or when putting together worksheets, others may include short interactive activities for students to do online and so on. The Tate Gallery website, for example, can be used by both teachers and students alike. The review below discusses it as a means of using ICT within the art lesson by students.

www.tate.org.uk/learning/learnonline

This site has several interactive activities for students of varying abilities. Although not highlighted as such, teachers may direct students to these activities according to levels of understanding and knowledge rather than those which seem obviously for students of a certain age. In this way, the activities are suitable for Key Stages 1–4. 'Tate Kids' is for students of primary age or lower ability. They may use this section of the site either individually or in pairs during the course of an art lesson or as an enrichment activity/homework. All require the student to interact with works of art by evaluating them, for example by solving puzzles or answering riddles, thus encouraging different ways of looking at art that promote depth of thought and discussion in fun ways.

Several skills can be built upon by engaging in these activities such as exploring and developing ideas, and if set for homework, the teacher can then assume prior learning and incorporate those new skills into subsequent lessons. There are practical activities, such as creating a collage based upon the work of Tony Cragg which can be used at the start of a lesson or again, as a homework project, enhancing the pupil's ability to make connections between their own and others' work. The pupil may then be asked to talk about and explain the thinking behind what they have done, thus making use of thinking skills and as a possible means of peer tutoring to other students in the class.

Literacy skills are enhanced via activities such as writing an online story based upon a given image from the Tate collection. Background information can be read about the image to allow for differentiated student approaches depending on the abilities of the group, or to assist the teacher when reviewing the task with students. The story forms an entry to an online competition but can be copied and pasted into a Word document to stick into sketchbooks with the image (which can be printed out directly from the site page) followed by subsequent artwork of the student's own composition based upon the theme (investigating and making).

Sketchbooks

The use of a sketchbook plays a vital part in enabling pupils to record observations and ideas, and collect visual evidence and information. The sketchbook provides the opportunity to:

- Collect thoughts and ideas.

- Create a personal, private and shared resource.

- Use for observational work, working out ideas, record studies from imagination.

- Use as a starting point from which to develop large-scale work.

- Use for experimenting with materials and techniques.

- Follow the established practice of artists.

- Contain evidence of gallery visits, working with artists etc.

- Work both inside and outside.

- Monitor progress and development.

- Develop a resource of ideas to inform further work.

The sketchbook may contain drawings, pieces of fabric, cuttings from magazines, postcards, mind maps, information about artists, computer-generated images, photographs and may include the use of a variety of graded pencils, pens, crayons, pastels, inks, a variety of paints etc.

The sketchbook is not a 'best' book but can, of course, contain finished pieces of work. For the pupil with SEN, as with all pupils, it may be a source of great pride and ownership.

Picasso said, 'Je suis le cahier' (*The Sketchbooks of Picasso*, 1996).

CHAPTER 5

Key Stage 3 Art and Design Projects for Use with Pupils with SEN

This chapter contains six art and design projects aimed at Key Stage 3. Each project has a keynote artist for reference, a planning sheet that includes learning objectives and outcomes, practical skills, visual elements and suggested resources, addressing investigating, making, knowledge and understanding. The projects also have exemplar photographs of pupil outcomes taken from real classroom situations.

The examples given in this chapter have been used with pupils with SEN in mainstream schools and are designed to identify and develop the artistic abilities of these pupils.

Project 1 – The Iron Man

Project 2 – Forms in a Landscape

Project 3 – Picasso, Plates and Portraiture

Project 4 – Identity

Project 5 – Flight

Project 6 – Water

There is an example of a starter project for the Iron Man, a homework project for Picasso, Plates and Portraiture and an activity sheet for Flight, which can be adapted for all projects.

The Art Planning Sheets may be inserted into the medium-term and long-term planning models. The medium-term planning sheet covers every aspect of planning for a Key Stage 3 art and design project.

Project 1 – The Iron Man

Key Stage 3 (3D and Mixed Media)

His eyes, like headlamps, glowed white, then red, then infra red searching the sea. ('The Iron Man', Ted Hughes)

This popular book by Ted Hughes may be a starting point for a variety of art projects in Key Stage 3.

The photographs of the artefacts, sculptures and paintings by artists such as Elizabeth Frink and Paolozzi may help in a discussion about the Iron Man, which may lead into the human figure/the fantastic and strange.

In sketchbooks

Children may collect pictures of objects made from iron or metal. Jot down in a variety of materials what they imagine the Iron Man looks like. Sketch from observation cogs, wheels, spoons, forks, bits of old clocks etc. A compilation of 'any old iron' could form a centre point of a 'still life' in the classroom. Colours of iron blues/greens as well as reds, browns etc.

In 3D form

An Iron Man could be assembled out of chicken wire and students then bring in bits of old metal to thread into the chicken wire, compiling an iron man. This could, of course, then be painted, drawn or modelled in clay and impressed with 'metal patterns'. These objects could be scanned into a computer and manipulated/repeated using software such as Photoshop, giving a contemporary 'feel' to old objects.

Prints

By drawing patterns into polystyrene, the prints completed in 'iron colours' could create a large iron man to be put on the classroom wall. Similarly, a collage of simple shapes cut out of textured card or thick paper could be inked up and printed onto a variety of coloured paper.

Paintings

Using the text as the imaginative starting point, develop a composition as part of the story. The actual text could be put onto a PC, exploring a variety of fonts and layouts, printed out and stuck onto the painted piece or painted over to add a graphic quality to the work.

Portraits

Half a self-portrait could change into half an iron man by metamorphosis. Examine paintings by Archimboldi, a Milanese painter of fantastic heads composed of fragments of landscape, vegetables and flowers. This could lead to a 'metal head' composition.

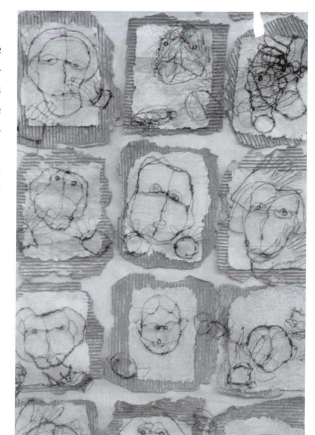

Assemblage

Pupils may build up their own Iron Man out of boxes. Use glue and sand to give an 'iron' textured surface before painting.

Identity – Who Am I?

The Iron Man theme may lead into a focus on personal identity: an attempt to bring together images of what makes me the person I am in terms of personality, my interests, my likes and dislikes.

A display of words and objects would make an interesting starting point for further discussion relating to the question of personal identity. ICT elements may also be incorporated here to animate the words, including the use of scanned or given images, or those taken by students using a digital camera (Photoshop or Flash animation).

Starter project

Taller than a house, the Iron Man stood at the top of the cliff, on the very brink, in the darkness.

The wind sang through his iron fingers. His great iron head, shaped like a dustbin but as big as a bedroom, slowly turned to the right, slowly turned to the left. His iron ears turned, this way, that way. He was hearing the sea. His eyes, like headlamps, glowed white, then red, then infra red, searching the sea. Never before had the Iron Man seen the sea.

He swayed in the strong wind that pressed against his back. He swayed forward, on the brink of the cliff.

- Using the text as an imaginative starting point, draw the Iron Man.

- Collect materials that have a metal texture to them, for example, corrugated card, tin foil, sandpaper etc. to create a collage.

- Bring into school an object made from metal, for example, old forks, bits of clock, cogs etc. to sketch from or scan or add to a chicken wire structure of an iron man.

- Make a list of words to describe the Iron Man thinking of colour, shape, texture, pattern and form.

- Research on the Internet, via the Tate website, one of the following artists: Elizabeth Frink, Giacometti, Anthony Caro or Anthony Gormley.

- Using the school digital camera, photograph a still life of rusty old objects and manipulate the images on Photoshop to create some abstract images.

The above ideas may be broken down as classroom activities, homework suggestions and starting points for prints, paintings, assemblage and plaster casts made from imprinted sand patterns of metal objects.

UNIT/LESSON	THE IRON MAN		
ART PLANNING SHEET	KEY STAGE 3	YEAR 7/8	DATE

TIMESCALE	VISUAL ELEMENTS:	PRACTICAL SKILLS:
	Pattern, texture, colour, line, tone, shape, form and space	Drawing, painting, printing, collage, textiles, 3D

STIMULUS

LEARNING OBJECTIVE(S) (INTENDED LEARNING OUTCOMES)

Pupils should be taught to:	Tick as appropriate		RESOURCES
		By manipulating wire, construct Iron Man/wire portraits. Develop drawing skills in pencil and wire, and understand some of the ideas behind Giacometti, Frink and Gormley sculptures. Key words for 3D and Iron Man – Ted Hughes	
Record responses, including observations of the natural and made environment.		1. Select key ideas from Iron Man to construct an iron man out of chicken wire. Pupils may bring old metal materials to thread through: spoons, nails etc.	Iron Man story – Ted Hughes Reproductions of sculptures of Gormley, Giacometti and Elizabeth Frink Drawing materials Soft wire/wire cutters Corrugated card Key words Painting materials Pencils Clay/plaster ICT materials
Gather resources and materials, using them to stimulate and develop ideas.		2. Draw in a variety of drawing materials, ink, pencil, charcoal etc. an iron man.	
Explore and use two- and three-dimensional media, working on a variety of scales.		3. With a mirror or photograph, draw a self-portrait. 4. Translate drawings into wire portraits.	
Review and modify their work as it progresses.		5. Mount on corrugated card. 6. Discuss the effectiveness of 'drawings' of Iron Man.	
Develop understanding of the work of artists, craftspeople and designers, applying knowledge to their own work.		Using 'key words' discuss sculptures by Anthony Gormley, Elizabeth Frink and Giacometti. **Parallel projects**	
Respond to and evaluate art, craft and design, including their own and others' work.		● Painting of an iron man/portrait ● Press print with polystyrene, clay, modelling materials ● Assemble/collage ● Sketchbook developments	

DEVELOPMENT/EVALUATION:

Artist for the Iron Man: Alberto Glacometti

Alberto Giacometti (1901–1966) was a Swiss sculptor and painter who at 15 enunciated a belief that was to remain with him all his life:

'Drawing is the basis of all the arts.'

His younger brother Bruno said,

'He had the habit of drawing everything around him. He always had pencil and paper in his hands. . .'

In his drawings of Henri Matisse, Giacometti proved what he had said as a teenager:

'he could do anything with this fabulous medium, drawing.'

However, it is his figurative sculptures, the tireless repetition of the same figures, the heads like knife blades, elongated bodies in bronze that are appropriate for 'Forms in a Landscape' or a striding Iron Man.

Walking Man II is in the Kröller-Müller Museum. It was commissioned for the plaza in front of the Chase Manhattan Bank in New York. Giacometti worked repeatedly on preparation studies, maquettes in plaster. He made two walking male figures as many as 40 times, modelling them and then destroying them again – he was rarely satisfied with his work.

Until now, and I think I will not change my mind, the most beautiful sculpture that I have found is neither Greek nor Roman, nor is it Renaissance, but Egyptian. . . The Egyptian sculptures have a grandeur, a rhythm of form, a perfect technique which no one has achieved since.

Artists whose work also complements the Iron Man project are as follows:

- Anthony Gormley   British sculptor (Angel of the North)
- Elizabeth Frink   British sculptor (Liverpool Cathedral)
- Gabriele Koch   Ceramicist (V&A)
- Eduardo Paolozzi   British sculptor and painter (British Library)

Project 2 – Forms in a Landscape

Key Stage 3 (Textiles)

Situation

Take a walk in a local landscape, park or school grounds to observe, collect, photograph and talk.

Colour:	Collect leaves, twigs, seeds, pebbles, feathers etc.
Line:	Take rubbings of pavement, walls, draw lines of a fence, gate, wall, leaves and trees.
Shape and pattern:	Photograph details, quick sketches of appropriate detail, e.g. patterns of leaves, trees etc.
Texture:	Collect different surface textures, take rubbings, and feel different surfaces.

Still life in classroom

- Plant forms, pebbles, wood, seeds, feathers etc.

- Paintings to illustrate theme

- Observation drawings, colour commentary, to lead into prints and paintings

- Colour swatches, pattern and line notes, shape outlines in a sketchpad

Key words

Colour	e.g. yellow ochre, burnt sienna
Texture	e.g. smooth, rough, spiky, angular
Line	e.g. straight, broken, curved, circular
Shape and pattern	e.g. spotted, striped, patterned, speckled, jagged
Materials	e.g. stone, wood, water, metal, plant form and soil
Mood	e.g. calm, relaxed, sad, happy, angry and tense, simplified forms, angular shapes, fragmented patterns etc.

Construct a willow triangle to develop a landscape theme

The pupils will develop 3D hangings based on a visit to the park and discussion of Michael Brennand-Wood, Andy Goldsworthy and other landscape artists' work.

- With the use of the following materials: willow, string, rubber bands, wools, leaves, twigs and drawing materials, the pupils will discuss how to construct their willow hangings.

- They may be based on a colour theme, e.g. greens to capture the colour of leaves, trees and plant forms and developing shapes and patterns found in these forms; greys, whites and blacks to represent pebbles and rocks etc.

- Pupils may collect a range of one colour (leaves, twigs, moss etc.) in a clear polythene sandwich bag to put in their sketchpads.

- The willow triangles may explore colour, shape, pattern, contain hanging objects, laminated leaves etc.

- The sculptures may be evaluated as they progress: what is the most effective willow hanging and why?

- Encourage pupils to look at other artists' work, e.g. Van Gogh, Richard Long, and discuss a way of representing their landscapes.

UNIT/LESSON	FORMS IN A LANDSCAPE	
ART PLANNING SHEET	KEY STAGE 3	YEAR 7/8 DATE

TIMESCALE	VISUAL ELEMENTS:	PRACTICAL SKILLS:
	Pattern, texture, colour, line, tone, shape, form and space	Drawing, painting, printing, collage, textiles, 3-D

STIMULUS

LEARNING OBJECTIVE(S) (INTENDED LEARNING OUTCOMES)

The students will develop 3D hangings based on a visit to the park/local landscape and discuss Michael Brennand-Wood and other artists' studies and will come to an understanding of weaving skills, structures and drawing from life.

Pupils should be taught to:	Tick as appropriate		RESOURCES
		1. Collect materials to put in sketchpad, rubbings, photographs, colour experiments.	Michael Brennand-Wood
			Andy Goldsworthy
Record responses, including observations of the natural and made environment.		2. Still life drawings, pastels and paintings of plant forms, pebbles and twigs.	Vincent Van Gogh: colour reproductions of their work
			Willow, string and wools, leaves, twigs and drawing/painting materials
Gather resources and materials, using them to stimulate and develop ideas.		3. Discuss ideas of making willow sculptures for hanging.	Key words
		4. Develop ideas exploring colour, shape and patterns developed across the willow triangle.	Sketchpad
Explore and use two- and three-dimensional media, working on a variety of scales.		5. Discuss the effectiveness of the willow hangings. Balance, colour and shapes. What was the most effective willow hanging and why?	
Review and modify their work as it progresses.		6. Encourage the children to look at other artists' work, e.g. Van Gogh, and discuss a way of representing his landscapes. Construct a willow triangle to develop a landscape theme.	
Develop understanding of the work of artists, craftspeople and designers, applying knowledge to their own work.			
Respond to and evaluate art, craft and design, including their own and others' work.			

DEVELOPMENT/EVALUATION:

Landscape Digital Project: Wastelands

The following is an example of a digital project worked with a mixed ability group of pupils, including pupils with SEN.

It was developed with artist Lara Almarcequi exhibiting at the Liverpool Biennial in September 2004 and in conjunction with Tate Liverpool.

- Pupils discussed Lara's work, exploring wasteland areas of the docklands of Rotterdam and Liverpool's old garden centre (video and photographic evidence).

- With digital cameras and sketchpads the pupils, accompanied by staff and Lara, explored four wasteland sites in Liverpool to record their findings.

- Working in small groups, back at the Tate, they discussed how to put a small Powerpoint display together capturing the essence of one of the sites.

- Words and sounds were added to the text to produce a five minute visual commentary of their visit.

- In the classroom, they created drawings, collages, poems and simple prints based on their findings and a still life of object finds, rusty locks, plants etc.

- Their ideas were as diverse as creating buildings for the derelict site, a colour manipulation using Photoshop of the digital images, layering of the images to create abstract designs.

The students recorded their thoughts about their findings and the future developments of the sites on a camcorder and a 30-minute DVD has been compiled by a local City Learning Centre. Each student has received a copy of the DVD.

Artist for Forms in a Landscape: Michael Brennand-Wood

Michael Brennand-Wood was born in Bury, Lancashire in 1952. He trained at Bolton College of Art, Manchester Polytechnic and Birmingham Polytechnic. He has won a range of awards; one in 1991 was the Art for Architecture Award given by the Royal Society of Art.

His work is mixed media/textile pieces, usually individual and wall hung. He uses wood, fabrics, paints, thread, paper and metal. His techniques employed include construction, interlacing, collage, stitchery and manipulation.

Recent exhibition: 2004 The Gallery, Ruthin Crafts Centre.

Michael's work is an exciting exploration of space, form and texture, examining the crossover between 'fine art installations' and the challenging boundaries of contemporary embroidery. Many of his pieces explore the themes of structure and architecture in an innovative way. The pattern and composition of Michael Brennand-Wood's work create a sense of movement and energy and may form a starting point for using pattern for decoration, on walls, carpets and clothes. By looking at patterns in nature (William Morris), patterns in architecture (The Alhambra Granada), pattern in a manuscript (Lindisfarne Gospel), pattern in painting (Wassily Kandinsky), the viewer may come to some understanding of Michael Brennand-Wood's intricately worked patterns in textiles.

Project 3 – Picasso, Plates and Portraiture

Key Stage 3

(Drawing, Mask Making and Print)

This project may be developed from a visit to a local art gallery to look at plates, or with reference to Picasso's ceramics and his portrait studies, from his Blue, Cubist, and Classical periods, or a collection of plates in the classroom (brought in by the students). A display of tribal masks may also be a good starting point.

Picasso painted, incised and modelled hundreds of plates with the face of a fawn. In Greek mythology, fawns, like satyrs and the god Pan, were half-goat, with a man's head and torso and a goat's legs, horns and tail. The fawn faces on Picasso's plates show every possible expression: smiling, gloomy, fierce, hilarious, sly and sad. Perhaps they represent a sort of serial self-portrait. Picasso made so many fawn plates that if seen together it might be imagined that he was attempting to paint Everyman, or the Man in the Street.

Picasso nearly always dated his work, especially his paintings and prints. He said, 'My work is like a diary. It's even dated like a diary.'

Introduce the stimulus material and explain the learning objectives.

- In sketchbooks collect faces from magazines, newspapers and, where possible, photos of friends and family.

- Take photographs of the pupils or supply mirrors.

- Use a variety of media to draw with: pencil, ink, biro, chalk and charcoal to create full portraits or profile views.

- Discuss Picasso's various portrait studies, from his Blue period, Cubist, Classical period and references to tribal masks.

- Use Photoshop or similar computer programme so students may scan, experiment and layer portraits.

- Photocopy, scan into a computer and reduce drawings to collage onto paper plates and strengthen by coating with Marvin medium.

- A Key Stage 3 development may be to build up a mask with papier mâché, paint and varnish. These can be mounted on a pole and displayed with a backdrop of self-portraits.

- Polystyrene prints incised with a biro using water-based printing inks and rollers could be an extension activity for this project.

The language of portraiture – faces, expressions and moods – may be recorded in the sketchpads, for example, happy, sad, angry, thoughtful, etc. and perhaps linked with colour. (This project may be linked to an Identity Project making hats.)

Homework suggestions

- Collect pictures from magazines of faces of old and young people. Create a collage of your collection in your sketchpad.

- Using a mirror, sketch a self-portrait or bring in a photograph of yourself or member of your family to scan in to manipulate the image with Photoshop.

- Research Picasso on the Internet, in the library or from a book in the art room. Choose a portrait to discuss and describe.

- From a postcard of a mask you have been given, create your own collage of a mask to show a mood: happy, sad, thoughtful, angry etc.

- Collect materials to create your carnival mask or hat: buttons, wools, a variety of papers, feathers, straws etc.

- Fold, pleat, tear, cut and hole-punch white paper to create different patterns and shapes for use on your mask and hat. Experiment with different joining techniques, i.e. paper clips, glue, stitching, threading and tying.

These homework suggestions run alongside teacher support in lessons, for example, providing pupils with the opportunity to handle simple masks and to consider and discuss methods used, introducing appropriate language for materials and tools. Encourage children to develop their own responses through observation and experimentation.

Assessment opportunities

- confidence and understanding in handling materials

- fine motor skills in controlling tools and materials

- use of appropriate vocabulary related to process

- use of more complex techniques throughout process

- e-sketchpad using a digital camera

Skills covered include basic mask-making techniques, portraiture, control of materials and tools.

UNIT/LESSON	PICASSO, PLATES AND PORTRAITURE		
ART PLANNING SHEET	**KEY STAGE 3**	**YEAR**	**DATE**
TIMESCALE	**VISUAL ELEMENTS:**		**PRACTICAL SKILLS:**
	Pattern, texture, colour, line, space, tone, shape, and form		Drawing, painting, collage, 3-D, ICT

STIMULUS

LEARNING OBJECTIVE(S) (INTENDED LEARNING OUTCOMES)

Pupils should be taught to:	Tick as appropriate	**By exploring Picasso's ceramics and portrait studies, students will create their own plates, prints and masks.**	**RESOURCES**
Record responses, including observations of the natural and made environment.		1. Collect reference materials in sketchbooks. 2. Students create portraits using a variety of media, including photographs. 3. Photocopy/scan drawings to collage onto paper plates. 4. Create a mask with papier mâché, paint and varnish. 5. Incise polystyrene and ink-up to make print portraits.	Picasso images, drawing materials Digital cameras Paper plates, ICT facilities, glue Printing inks, rollers, paper Key words Carnival images
Gather resources and materials, using them to stimulate and develop ideas.		**Parallel project** • Exploring identity through making hats, relating this to Carnival time.	
Explore and use two- and three-dimensional media, working on a variety of scales.			
Review and modify their work as it progresses.			
Develop understanding of the work of artists, craftspeople and designers, applying knowledge to their own work.			
Respond to and evaluate art, craft and design, including their own and others' work.			

DEVELOPMENT/EVALUATION:

Artist for plates and portraiture: Picasso

Picasso was born in Malaga, Spain on 25 October 1881. During the early part of his life, he lived in Barcelona and trained at the Art Academy in Madrid. By the age of 17 his artistic output was superior to that of his professors so he abandoned his training and by 1901 was living in Paris. In his early years in Paris, he painted canvases that came later to be known as his Blue period, since they were dominated by shades of blue and green.

In 1907 Picasso's work became influenced by African sculpture and he frequently visited the ethnographic museum in Paris. In his sketchbooks leading to 'Les Demoiselles d'Avignon' can be seen drawings that evoke an ancient Mediterranean civilisation with symmetrical, geometric forms suggesting early Egyptian wall painting or Greek vase decoration. These ideas led onto the multi-viewpoint perspectives of early Cubism. In his drawing 'Head of a man', the features are not seen from one perspective but from many.

Between 1912 and 1914 Picasso made, alongside Braque, the first 'collage'. These collages consisted of cut-out shapes to identify a violin, guitar, bottle, fruit etc. Music sheets could be music sheets, and wallpaper could be wallpaper. Through cut-out collage Picasso created the illusion of space. Small constructions like 'Guitar' built outwards into actual space.

After the First World War Picasso revived traditional representation. This was called his Neo Classical period. Helped technically by his sculptor friend Julio Gonzales, he worked with wire, metal sheets and found objects to produce assembled sculpture, for example, 'Head of a Woman 1930'. This work had a surrealist connection.

Considered to be the most famous painting of the twentieth century is 'Guernica', a large monochrome picture, which describes the horrors of war after the bombing of Guernica, a small Spanish town, in 1937.

After the war until his death on 8 April 1973, Picasso lived and worked in Paris and the south of France. During this nearly 80 year period he designed stained glass windows, sculpted in clay, cast in bronze, experimented with found objects, painted portraits of Claude, his son, and Paloma, his daughter. His work was a continual experimentation with paint, printing and three-dimensional form and when he died in 1973 he left some 175 sketchbooks (almost 7,000 drawings) which were the inspiration for his completed works.

In old age Picasso was fond of remarking that

'*Painting is stronger than I am. It can make me do whatever it wants.*'

He inscribed the words on the inside back cover of a late sketchbook, and when he did so he was in a sense writing his own epitaph.

Project 4 – Identity

Key Stage 3 (Hats 3D)

For me, the image of the head is a good place to put ideas and sensations. After all, everything goes on in your head. If you think of past civilisations there are marvellous head sculptures. Everyone's emotions are in their face. (Elizabeth Frink)

All mythologies contain many-headed creatures, animals, men, spirits, gods and goddesses. Each of these heads is a manifestation peculiar to its owner. The naga, a seven-headed serpent, expresses the symbolism of that number. Symbolic arithmetic combines with the symbolism peculiar to the many-headed creature. Janus had two faces so that he could look forwards and backwards, into the past and into the future. Horapollon states that 'in Egypt the coupling of two heads, the one male the other female, was a symbol of protection against evil spirits.'

'Headdress' is a word that can mean both what one puts on one's head, and also the way the hair is dressed. Hair or head-dressing could become a distinguishing mark of profession, caste, rank, age or of the ideal and even of unconscious tendencies. To wear a special headdress is to state a difference, to distinguish a particular rank. A ceremonial headdress may symbolise a magic power.

The hat is a symbol of identity. As Jung says, to change one's hat is to change one's ideas and view of the world. Helmets are symbols of invisibility, invulnerability and power. Key Stage 3 pupils begin to consider their own identity. A project beginning with portraiture and leading to constructing hats is an interesting way to explore the theme of identity and individual creativity.

Visit an art gallery, exploring the theme of portraiture. Make a display of a variety of portrait examples in the classroom.

Portraiture – the human head – some related artists

Identity/Disguise	Da Vinci, Picasso, Modigliani, Magritte, Dubuffet, Khalo, Munch, Frink
Identity/Status	Ancient tomb paintings, effigies, Van Eyck, Holbein, Renaissance portraits, Reynold, Gainsborough, Van Dyck, Frans Hals, Vermeer, Hogarth, Klimt, Rego
Expressionist	El Greco, Goya, Van Gogh, Dubuffet, Grosz, Lautrec, Kokoschka, Beckmann, Dix, Munch, Soutine, Bacon, Auerbach, Kossoff, Schiele, Appel, Kollwitz, De Kooning, Giacometti, Bellany
Series	Gericault (portraits from the asylum), Rembrant (self-portraits), Andy Warhol, Bacon

Movement	Duchamp, Picasso, Balla, Bacon
Relationships	Henry Moore (family groups), Brancussi, Schiele, Cassat, Morrisot
Photography	Cameron, Beaton, Hockney, Sherman, Cartier-Bresson
Surrealism	Archimboldo, The Art of Caricature, Kahlo, Dali
Fantastic/Strange	Magritte, Carrington
Identity – Who am I?	Van Gogh, Rembrandt, Picasso, Chris Offili, Joseph Cornell, Gwen John

This project takes as its focus personal identity, not as a straightforward self-portrait, which is a painting, drawing or sculpture, but as an attempt to bring together images of what makes me the person I am in terms of my personality, my interests, my likes and dislikes etc. Initially pupils can record these things in words. They can collect objects and images of the things they like:

- mirrors or photographs of pupils to develop a self-portrait in pencil, ink, paint and collage;

- design a hat or headpiece to describe the pupils' own interests;

- media: card, straws, paper, paint, textiles and ICT.

Learning objectives/skills

- Develop pupils' observational skills.

- Develop pupils' skills in the selection and use of appropriate materials and colours.

- Develop pupils' skills in the application of paint and working in a 3D form.

- Develop an understanding of the way in which various artists have represented faces and expressions.

- Make a collection and place in a sketchpad 'hats', fashion statements, non-Western cultures, carnival and working 'headgear'.

- Alternatively pupils could design 'an artist's hat'.

UNIT/LESSON	IDENTITY		
ART PLANNING SHEET	**KEY STAGE 3**	**YEAR 7/8/9**	**DATE**
TIMESCALE	**VISUAL ELEMENTS:**		**PRACTICAL SKILLS:**
	Line, colour, texture, pattern, form and shape		Drawing, painting, collage, textiles, 3D

STIMULUS

LEARNING OBJECTIVE(S) (INTENDED LEARNING OUTCOMES)

Pupils should be taught to:	Tick as appropriate	**Pupils will build upon previous experience by extending their range of skills. To learn that clothes reflect different cultures and that materials can be manipulated to express an idea/identity. To demonstrate and understand the skills of joining and fastening.**	RESOURCES
		1. Pupils select a self-portrait that they have previously completed. This may have been in ink, paint, collage or computer-generated.	Carnival images, fashion hats (e.g. Philip Treacy)
Record responses, including observations of the natural and made environment.		2. In sketchpads, pupils make a collection of hats, fashion statements, non-Western culture's carnival and working headgear.	Access to ICT, images and words
Gather resources and materials, using them to stimulate and develop ideas.		3. Pupils design a hat or headpiece to describe the pupil's own interests (Research – images that describe personality, likes and dislikes). These can be recorded in words. Objects and images may also be collected which will help to develop the design.	Paper, card, tissue, straws, fabric, PVA glue, hole punch, etc.
Explore and use two- and three-dimensional media, working on a variety of scales.		4. Pupils are provided with a selection of materials, e.g. card, straws, paper, paint, fabrics and create their 3D hat design. Skills will involve joining, fastening, manipulation of materials and imagination.	
Review and modify their work as it progresses.		5. Alternatively, pupils could design and make a 'Picasso' hat.	
Develop understanding of the work of artists, craftspeople and designers, applying knowledge to their own work.			
Respond to and evaluate art, craft and design, including their own and others' work.			
DEVELOPMENT/EVALUATION:			

Critical study reference for identity: Caribbean Masquerade

The Caribbean festivals are a mixture of the traditions of a range of cultures: Arawak, Carib, European, African and Asian. Before the arrival of Christopher Columbus in 1492, the Caribbean Islands were inhabited by Indians from the Carib and Arawak tribes.

The fusion of cultures has produced a unique art form: the Caribbean Carnival, also known as 'Mas'. Two major Mas festivals are celebrated: the pre-Lenten Carnival and the Jonkonnu or Christmas Masquerade.

In Europe, pre-Lenten celebrations in, for example, Germany and Venice explore the anonymity of masquerades. Freedom of comment and behaviour is made possible through personal 'disguise'. The Notting Hill and Leeds Carnivals have led to an industry of Mas designers in Britain.

The Jonkonnu is a major celebration in Jamaica and the Bahamas and is a street festival. This festival is an interesting occasion to develop in the classroom; it has links with architecture, for the Jonkonnu player wears a wire screen mask and a house balanced on his head.

Bands of Jonkonnu Masquerades performed before the great houses of the plantations from the beginning of the eighteenth century. The characters wore a variety of costumes as they mimed and danced, accompanied by a small musical band.

The Jonkonnu festival derives its name from the mime character Jonn Canue, thought to be based on the successful eighteenth-century merchant John Conny. The main character always wears a mask. The house is constructed of pasteboard and coloured papers, usually highly ornamented with beads, tassels, spangles and pieces of looking glass. The African practice of assemblage (combining different materials and objects into a three-dimensional work of art) is incorporated into Jonkonnu costumes. As well as shells, feathers, seeds, bones, horns, leaves and raffia, nowadays manufactured materials such as plastic flowers, cut-outs from magazines, mirrors, playing cards, glitter, sequins, fabric and lighting effects are incorporated into costumes.

Carnival in Europe has a fascinating history, from animal masked dancers in cave paintings, to Greek Carnivals in honour of Dionysus, the Jewish Carnival Purim, Medieval Europe's 'Feast of the Fools'; the characters of Punchinello, Pierrot, Harlequin and Columbine are just a few references to this period of celebration.

The word 'Carnival' comes from the Latin *Carnem levare* meaning literally to put away (i.e. not to eat meat). The last day of Roman Catholic European Carnival is known as Shrove Tuesday or Mardi Gras and the first day of Lent as Ash Wednesday.

Today Mas themes confront issues such as pollution, world conservation, equality, poverty, homelessness and economic recession. They celebrate the richness of multicultural society, the valuing of art and cultural tradition, freedom of expression, goodwill, community spirit, and innovations of new design and technology.

Key art works

The Fight between Carnival and Lent	1559	Pieter Breughel
Surrounded by Masks	1889	James Ensor
Three Musicians	1921	Pablo Picasso
A Carnival Evening	1886	Henri Rousseau

The work of Inigo Jones (1573–1652), English architect and stage designer. (References to the Jonkonnu taken from The Visual Learning Foundation publication *Masquerade* (ISBN 0 9531329 00)).

Project 5 – Flight

Key Stage 3 (3D: Kites)

This kite project is based upon the story of Daedalus and Icarus and a poem by W.H. Auden, 'Musée des Beaux Arts'. The following list of work could be used throughout the project as resource and reference material, appropriate to the abilities of students:

Pieter Breughel – Landscape with the Fall of Icarus (1555–58)

Nike of Samothrace – Classical Greek sculpture (400BC)

'Icarus by Mobile' – poem by Gareth Owen

'Gulls' – poem by Ted Hughes

'Breughel in Naples' – poem by Dannie Abse

Leonardo Da Vinci – Notebooks on flight (1453–1519)

Albrecht Dürer – Wing Study (1512)

Elisabeth Frink – Wing/Flight Sculptures

Photographs of kites and historical notes

Edwin Aldrin – Apollo II, 20 July 1969

Butterfly images

Audubon paintings

In sketchbooks

A visit to a local museum's Natural History Department may yield interesting direct observational work from stuffed birds, butterflies, moths, etc. and pieces could be built upon using collage, paint or other media, possibly in situ with the museum's permission. Students may also collect pictures of things that fly, living or non-living, and then proceed to make sketches/collages from these images.

Back in school, the teacher may set up a still life of assorted kites, for example traditional, high-tech, Chinese – students can make drawings or collages from this arrangement that emphasise colour, pattern and form.

In 2D/3D form

Students can develop their ideas and designs for their own kites (individually or within a group) either on paper with pencils, acrylic or watercolour paints, inks and brushes, or three-dimensionally with materials such as tissue paper and thin wire. This work, once completed, could then be scanned into a computer and manipulated using software such as Photoshop, to extend design, colour

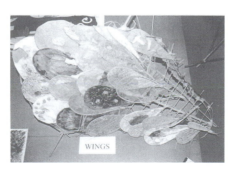

or pattern ideas. Once the pieces are printed out, they can be used to form a collage or torn/cut up to form part of the kite to be made later.

Once this stage has been completed, the teacher and students should discuss the effectiveness of wings/kites, balance, colour, shape and materials in order to inform their next steps into 3D. Music such as Stravinsky's 'The Firebird' could be played to students to extend discussion on colour, with thoughts jotted down in sketchbooks.

3D kites

The kites may be developed using willow or thin wire to form the underlying structure. Tie and dye techniques on cotton, based on the students' designs/butterfly shapes, etc., can form the 'skin' of the kite; alternatively batik techniques may be used on cotton fabric or paper and while the wax is still wet, students may embed items relating to flight such as sycamore wings, small feathers, dandelion 'clocks' or torn parts of their own drawings of butterfly wings or their digital images. The fabric or paper can be either stitched or glued to the structure using PVA glue. Before embarking on the final kite, students may wish to experiment with a variety of techniques in sketchbooks.

These kites are for artistic purposes and are not meant to fly. Should this be important to students, due consideration should be given to the materials used and their durability out of doors.

Additional activities

1 The pupils may be given an excerpt from the story of Icarus (large print where appropriate) and then they underline or write out a list of words related to flight, e.g. feathers, blue sky etc. This could be done using a computer/sketchpad.

2 Collect pictures of flight, e.g. space rockets, birds, dandelion clocks, flying fish, and collage them into a sketchpad or scan them into a computer.

3 Design a flying machine with the help of photocopies of Leonardo Da Vinci's designs.

4 Using wax resist (batik wax or candle patterns) experiment with dyes and inks to create resist patterns.

5 Design a kite, based on butterfly or bird patterns, choosing a colour theme: blues/purples: or yellow/oranges/reds etc.

6 Make a kite out of:

   - willow, tie and dyed cotton;

   - diamond-shaped card painted and/or collaged, or wax resist;

   - a collage of photocopies, glued and coated on polythene and peeled off when dry to create a kite shape to be attached to a simple wood frame, willow or dowelling.

Create a tail for the kite using the most appropriate materials to match the kite design, tied cotton pieces, paper or torn polythene bags.

UNIT/LESSON	FLIGHT		
ART PLANNING SHEET	**KEY STAGE 3**	**YEAR**	**DATE**
TIMESCALE	**VISUAL ELEMENTS:**		**PRACTICAL SKILLS:**
	Pattern, texture, colour, line, tone, space, tone, shape and form		Drawing, painting, printing, collage, textiles, 3D

STIMULUS

LEARNING OBJECTIVE(S) (INTENDED LEARNING OUTCOMES)

Research, design and build a kite based on direct observations of butterflies etc. and/or the story of Icarus.

	Tick as appropriate		RESOURCES
Pupils should be taught to:		1. Pupils familiarise themselves with the story of Icarus and related images.	Painting by Breughel (Landscape with the Fall of Icarus)
Record responses, including observations of the natural and made environment.		2. Collect materials/pictures to put in sketchpad relating to flight.	
		3. Pupils make observational drawings from natural forms; a visit to a Natural History Museum or equivalent may be appropriate.	Batik on paper, tie and dye
Gather resources and materials, using them to stimulate and develop ideas.		4. Pupils experiment with a range of dyes and resist techniques or trapping small objects between tissue paper with PVA glue, developing the shapes, colours and patterns of the natural forms.	Garden canes, willow, dowelling, etc. String, twine, tie and dye offcuts
Explore and use two- and three-dimensional media, working on a variety of scales.		5. Design a kite (using a simple crossbar structure) that emphasises shapes, colours and patterns from direct observations.	
Review and modify their work as it progresses.		6. Pupils make the kite using tie and dye on cotton and either wrapped around the willow structure or stretched round a card kite shape. Tail of the kite may be constructed from twine, ribbon, cotton strips, etc. and could be experimental rather than traditional	
Develop understanding of the work of artists, craftspeople and designers, applying knowledge to their own work.		7. When evaluating the work, the effectiveness of the balance, shape and colour/material usage may be discussed. Further exploration and discussion could also be made with colour and mood as represented in music such as Stravinsky's 'Firebird' and the Phoenix myth.	
Respond to and evaluate art, craft and design, including their own and others' work.			

DEVELOPMENT/EVALUATION:

Musée des Beaux Arts

About suffering they were never wrong,

The Old Masters: how well they understood

Its human position; how it takes place

While someone else is eating or opening a window or just
  walking dully along;

How, when the aged are reverently, passionately waiting

For the miraculous birth, there always must be

Children who did not specially want it to happen, skating

On a pond at the edge of the wood:

They never forgot

That even the dreadful martyrdom must run its course

Anyhow in a corner, some untidy spot

Where the dogs go on with their doggy life and the torturer's
  horse

Scratches its innocent behind on a tree.

In Breughel's *Icarus*, for instance: how everything turns away

Quite leisurely from the disaster; the ploughman may

Have heard the splash, the forsaken cry,

But for him it was not an important failure; the sun shone

As it had to on the white legs disappearing into the green

Water; and the expensive delicate ship that must have seen

Something amazing, a boy falling out of the sky,

Had somewhere to get to and sailed calmly on.

W.H. Auden

Daedalus and Icarus

Daedalus, a Greek from Athens, was most widely known throughout the Ancient World as a craftsman, inventor and artist. He perfected the art of sculpture, making his works extremely lifelike. His fame spread across the whole of Greece and reached Africa. The Egyptians worshipped him as a god.

In those days, young men learned their trade and skills as apprentices to older men who were very experienced in their craft. Daedalus took on his sister's son, Perdix, as an apprentice and taught him all he knew. Soon Perdix became a better craftsman than Daedalus and this made Daedalus very jealous. So much so that he tried to kill Perdix by pushing him off a high tower. But Perdix was saved by the goddess Athene, who turned him into a partridge so that he could fly away before hitting the ground.

Daedalus was found guilty of attempting to murder Perdix and he fled to Crete with his young son, Icarus. After many years serving the king there, who thought he was a wonderful craftsman, Daedalus decided it was time to go back to his homeland of Athens. But how could he and Icarus build a ship for the long return journey without drawing attention to themselves? They came up with a daring idea – to make wings for themselves so that they could fly to Athens just like the birds!

First, Daedalus and Icarus collected as many feathers as they could find from birds of all sizes and shapes and arranged them on the ground so that they looked like very large bird's wings. They used wax to stick all the feathers together and then they could bend and curve them so that they fitted better. Daedalus tried them out first, jumping from nearby slopes to practise until he felt he was ready to make the flight back to Athens. He helped Icarus to make some more wings for himself and together they rehearsed their flying techniques.

Eventually it was time to make the flight. The sun was shining and the wind was blowing gently in the right direction. Daedalus told his son, 'Follow me and do as I do. If you fly too low then the spray from the sea will weigh your wings down; if you fly too high the heat from the sun will melt your wings – either way, you will die. Take care. I'll go first and may the gods be with you.' With that Daedalus took off and flew straight towards Athens. Icarus then followed, but as he got up into the blue sky he forgot all his father's advice and started swooping high, then low. He was so excited! He decided to see how high he could fly and before very long he felt his wings getting hotter and the wax starting to melt, trickling down his back. He panicked and sank towards the sea as fast as he could but it was not fast or cold enough for the wax to set again and Icarus plunged into the sea . . . to his death.

Their flight back to Athens had been so carefully and secretly planned that no one expected to see two men flying in the sky and therefore no one even noticed Icarus fall. Deadalus noticed too late that his son was no longer behind him. He flew back but it was too late to save his son. Desperately sad, he had to carry on on his own, leaving the debris of the melted wings floating on the sea.

Project 6 – Water

Key Stage 3 (Print)

This print project is based upon the work of David Hockney and his depictions of water. Students will explore the theme of water by looking at Hockney's paintings to create a large class or group wall hanging that comprises students' responses to the theme in print using a variety of techniques appropriate to the abilities of the individual student.

The following could be collected by the teacher or set as research homeworks for the students at the start of the project:

David Hockney information (life, works, etc.)

David Hockney images of water (e.g. 'A Bigger Splash' 1967; 'Water Pouring into Swimming Pool, Santa Monica' 1964)

Action words

Music (e.g. Handel's 'Water' music, Debussy's 'La Mer')

Literature relating to water (mermaids/myth, etc.)

Science links

Humanities (religious symbolic meanings of water, etc.)

In sketchbooks

Students should experiment with colour to create a wide range of blue and green shades. Experiment with lines to gain the most effective representation of water or try mixing PVA glue with paint and apply to card with brushes, combs or corrugated card to see various effects and to create surface pattern. Stick finished experiments into sketchbooks to create a reference for building upon.

Try ripping a variety of papers in appropriate colours. Using paint, ink, pastel and crayons, develop work from interpretations of the word 'splash'.

Other techniques may include using water-based inks and brushes, procion dyes on thin or sheer fabric or tracing paper, or layering of watercolours to create a sheer effect. The layering process can be taken onto a PC or Apple Mac using Photoshop processes of layering/use of transparency, utilising scanned-in work created by the students.

Students may then develop their ideas for a simple print that can be created using similar techniques to those of applying paint – polyprinting, where a biro is used to draw a design or simple pattern onto polystyrene and this is then inked up and printed onto assorted types of paper.

In 2D/3D form

Students should discuss their ideas on the production of a hanging that is made up of individual prints. Annotated sketches may be created in sketchpads. The prints could be suspended using garden canes or attached to a transparent material such as polythene. Consideration should be given to the overall 'look' of the hanging – does it create an image of water?

Development

A development of this project may be to explore the colour in more depth, for example, by building a compartmentalised box to hold 'experiments' with blue in a variety of media (see photograph).

Evaluation of work in progress

Does the printing process create clear patterns? What was the most effective 'splash' material/method? How effective is torn paper in creating a 'swimming pool' effect? Compare and contrast with cellophane collages.

Evaluation

Did all the students contribute to the hanging and did they see individual contributions work towards the whole image?

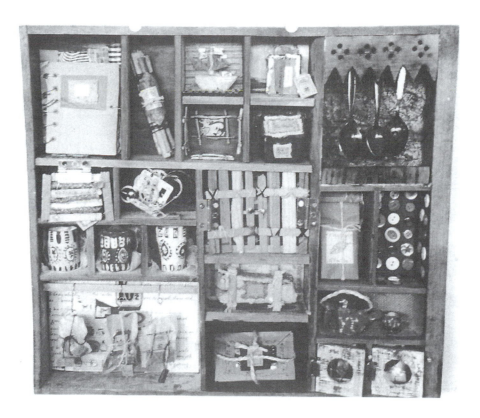

UNIT/LESSON	WATER		
ART PLANNING SHEET	**KEY STAGE 3**	**YEAR 7/8**	**DATE**

TIMESCALE	**VISUAL ELEMENTS:**	**PRACTICAL SKILLS:**
	Pattern, texture, colour, line, tone, shape, form and space	Drawing, painting, printing, collage, textiles, 3D

STIMULUS

LEARNING OBJECTIVE(S) (INTENDED LEARNING OUTCOMES)

	Tick as appropriate	Develop a frieze based on one of the Hockney's swimming pool paintings to explore the theme of water through colour, texture, shape and pattern employing a variety of media.	RESOURCES
Pupils should be taught to:			
Record responses, including observations of the natural and made environment.		1. Discuss some examples of David Hockney's water-related paintings (swimming pools, showers, garden sprays, etc). Talk a little about his life. Set up a still life related to water eg, blue swimming costume, goggles, water, seaweed, photographs of water – sea, lakes, etc.	Examples of Hockney's paintings and self-portraits Still life materials Blue/green theme photographs, pictures of water, lakes, seas, etc. Moods of water: rough, calm, etc. Printing ink and rollers, polystyrene Paint, ink, pastel crayons, variety of papers
Gather resources and materials, using them to stimulate and develop ideas.		2. Explore the colour of water by creating collages of torn paper into squares. Students are given a variety of blues, greens, purples, and whites – also a variety of surface textures.	
Explore and use two- and three-dimensional media, working on a variety of scales.		3. By indenting polystyrene squares with a variety of patterns taken from his paintings, print in a variety of blues, greens and purples.	
Review and modify their work as it progresses.		4. Using paint, ink, pastel and crayons, develop interpretations of the word 'splash'.	
Develop understanding of the work of artists, craftspeople and designers, applying knowledge to their own work.			
Respond to and evaluate art, craft and design, including their own and others' work.			

DEVELOPMENT/EVALUATION:

Artist for Water: David Hockney

David Hockney was born in Bradford, Yorkshire in 1937. He attended Bradford College of Art 1959–1962. He has worked in a variety of media and is one of the best known of all British artists. At the beginning of his career in the 1960s, he was associated with what is known as Pop Art. David had spent much of his time in California, USA where he now has his home. Many of his artworks relate to the lifestyle he lives in Los Angeles, e.g. swimming pools, Californian landscapes, photographic collages of friends, and landmarks in America, for example the Brooklyn Bridge.

Hockney employs a wide variety of media, such as acrylic, oils, pastels, pencil, screen-printing, paper making, etching, photography and lithography. He works with computer technology and has designed for the stage and opera.

David Hockney's favourite artist and greatest influence in his work is Picasso.

I do believe that art should be deep pleasure and a part of everyone's life. I do not think we can live without art of some form. I think I would be quite mad without it.

Summary: Progression of art skills

The projects outlined cover all learning styles and a variety of skills: drawing, painting, printing, collage, 3D, textiles, information gathering and ICT. Progression in these skills is indicated below. Teachers will be able to select and differentiate the aspects most appropriate to their pupils' needs and facilitate access to learning by:

- Encouraging pupils to use all available senses and experiences through art, craft and design.

- Planning for full participation by ensuring all projects provide a range of activities appropriate to pupils' diverse learning needs.

- Helping children to manage their behaviour by planning and providing for a range of appropriate practical activities that ensure each child can achieve, participate in the curriculum, and raise self-esteem and motivation.

- Helping pupils to manage their emotions by nurturing a sense of achievement – process is equally as important as the final outcome. All aspects of art, craft and design provide a vehicle for expressing feelings, thoughts and ideas.

- Allowing teachers the discretion to provide pupils with appropriate learning activities to award levels from P1 to Key Stage 3 and above. Even the slightest progress may enhance the confidence of pupils.

Drawing skills

Experimental: Mark-making using a variety of materials, working on a range of surfaces and size.

Project: A specific image may be chosen at this point, e.g. self-portrait in the Picasso project. Links here with a range of artists.

Sketchbooks: Pupils may extend their skills by introducing further opportunities to draw from a still life – natural and man-made objects – e.g. the Iron Man project.

Information-gathering: This could incorporate aspects of ICT in the research of an artist and/or a variety of drawing software.

Refining skills: To address composition, the concepts of perspective, line, tone and texture and pupil selection of appropriate materials, e.g. pencil, charcoal, biro, ink, etc.

Examples of works of art: Pupils make drawings from artworks seen in galleries, books, posters, etc. and make connections between these and their own work.

Drawing may obviously be the starting point for textiles, painting, printing and 3D.

Painting skills

Experimental: Explore a range of mark-making with paint using card, brushes, sticks, sponges and fingers, etc. Recognition of primary and secondary colours, colour games, mixing different consistencies of paint adding sand, glue, etc.

Project: Pupils may paint from natural forms, events, a figure, or fantastic and strange and from the abstract, using similar starting points as artists, e.g. water/Hockney project.

Sketchbooks: Can be used to experiment further with other paints such as watercolours, ink and wash, etc. and on a variety of surfaces such as torn paper. These may also be used to record from direct experience to inform paintings.

Information-gathering: Pupils may research artists on the Internet or collect images in order to become familiar with a variety of artists' styles.

Refining skills: Pupils may choose different methods, scale and colour to express mood and feeling and to explore the effect of light, colour, texture and tone.

Examples of works of art: A reproduction of a painting may be a vehicle for developing appropriate oral and literacy skills.

Printing skills

Experimental: Pupils may experiment with paint, printing inks and textured objects, e.g. hand-printing, corrugated card, vegetables, sponges, sticks and rollers, to explore the three main methods of printmaking, i.e. direct printing, incised printing and stencil/mask printing.

Project: Incise printing – cutting away a pattern using press-print to create surface texture/pattern for Iron Man project, for example.

Sketchbooks: Pupils record their techniques and keep samples in sketchbooks throughout, for example the variety of materials that may be used in collograph – foil, string, wallpaper, etc.

Information-gathering: Pupils research the different types of printmaking, e.g. Japanese woodcuts and artists, African woodcuts, William Morris stencils, Dürer etchings.

Refining skills: Pupils may transfer images onto fabric and/or iron-on computer-generated images; if equipment is available, this could be developed into screenprinting onto different surfaces.

Examples of works of art: The Flight project may explore Japanese prints to develop and decorate kite designs.

Health and Safety

Teachers must consider health and safety implications in all aspects of printing, e.g. protective clothing and safe use of tools and equipment.

3D

Experimental: Pupils experiment by manipulating different materials such as clay, plasticine, dough, sand and plaster, and develop an appropriate vocabulary. They may explore form, shape and pattern through incising and constructing. Note: The handling and manipulation of tools and materials requires fine motor skills.

Project: In both the Iron Man and Flight projects, pupils experiment with joining and fastening techniques. Construction and deconstruction could be explored here linking with the appropriate artists, e.g. Anthony Gormley, photographs of Carnival headdresses, etc.

Sketchbooks: Pupils may use their sketchbooks to gather information on 3D artists and also to record and explore construction techniques – cutting, bending, sticking and slotting.

Information-gathering: Pupils should be encouraged to research a wide range of 3D forms, e.g. kites, natural sculptures, wall hangings, Carnival costumes, terracotta army, etc.

Refining skills: Create 3D forms using a wider variety of materials such as modroc, papier mâché and wire armatures (Portraiture and Iron Man projects).

Examples of works of art: Carnival hat project may look at Aztec designs of hats, North American Indian headdresses or the paintings of Piero della Francesca.

Health and Safety

Teachers must consider health and safety implications in all aspects of 3D working, e.g. sharp wire, cutters and construction techniques and adequate ventilation when using plaster and clay.

Textiles

Experimental: Teachers should introduce pupils to a wide variety of fabrics and discuss the feel and look of them using appropriate vocabulary. Examples may be shown of printed, woven and embroidered textiles from both Western and non-Western cultures.

Project: Forms in the Landscape project utilises a variety of materials such as string, wood, seeds, dyed fabric, etc. Pupils are encouraged to experiment with these to create simple weaving and collage work.

Sketchbooks: Pupils may collect natural materials, e.g. sycamore wings or leaves and a variety of papers such as handmade or textured. They could explore simple stitching techniques and wax-resist experiments, i.e. candle wax and inks.

Information-gathering: Pupils could research different printed textiles from other cultures (India, Africa, Indonesia) and contemporary artists such as Michael Brennand-Wood, making sketches and developing their own designs where appropriate. Sandwich bags could be used to collect items of similar colour (Water project).

Refining skills: For the Forms in the Landscape project, pupils will extend the range of materials to be used including willow constructions and may work on a larger scale, perhaps in small groups. It is essential that pupils explore, experiment and develop their use of materials, by ripping, tearing, twisting, weaving, sewing and collage.

Examples of works of art: From the Bayeux Tapestry to African tie and dye and ceremonial costume right up to contemporary textiles that may be shown in an art gallery setting.

Health and Safety

Teachers must consider health and safety implications in all aspects of textile work, e.g. safe use of batik tools and a wax pot, needles and use of dyes.

CHAPTER 6

Real Pupils in Real Classrooms

This chapter introduces some case studies of pupils with some examples of projects that can support the teaching of art and design.

Kuli, Year 8	Hearing impairment
Harry, Year 7	Dyslexia
Megan, Year 10	Wheelchair user
Steven, Year 8	Emotional Behavioural and Social Difficulties
Matthew, Year 9	Cognitive and learning difficulties
Bhavini, Year 9	Visual impairment
Susan, Year 10	Complex difficulties, Asperger's Syndrome
Jenny, Year 7	Down's Syndrome

Kuli (Hearing impairment)

Kuli has significant hearing loss. He has some hearing in his right ear but is heavily reliant on his hearing aid and visual cues ranging from lip reading to studying body language and facial expression to get the gist and tone of what people are saying. He often misses crucial details. Reading is a useful alternative input and his mechanical reading skills are good but he does not always get the full message because of language delay. He has problems with new vocabulary and with asking and responding to questions.

Now in Year 8, he follows the same timetable as the rest of his class for most of the week but he has some individual tutorial sessions with a teacher of the deaf to help with his understanding of the curriculum and to focus on his speech and language development. This is essential but it does mean that he misses some classes so he is not always up to speed with a subject.

He has a good sense of humour but appreciates visual jokes, more than ones which are language-based. He is very literal and is puzzled by all sorts of idioms. He was shocked when he heard that someone had been 'painting the town red' as he thought this was an act of vandalism! Even when he knows what he wants to say he does not always have the words or structures to communicate accurately what he knows.

Everyone is very pleasant and quite friendly to him but he is not really part of any group and quite often misunderstands what other kids are saying. He has a Learning Assistant which again marks him out as different. He gets quite frustrated because he always has ideas that are too complex for his expressive ability. He can be very sulky and has temper tantrums.

Strategies

- Kuli needs to know what is coming up in the next few lessons so he can prepare the vocabulary and get some sense of the main concepts in order for him to follow what is being said. He could be given a copy of the lesson outline which should highlight key words, skills and techniques, etc.

- A good teaching assistant will find ways of displaying information visually using other pieces of artwork, images, signs, symbols, sign language, mime, animations on a computer, etc.

- Classroom displays should be changed to illustrate the new topic and the teacher should find relevant examples of past pupils' work for exemplification of expected outcomes.

- Key words and formal elements can be displayed imaginatively so that Kuli does not have to rely on the teacher explaining verbally, e.g. the word 'texture' on a textured background, the word 'tone' on a shaded background and so on. These could be cut out and strung together to form a mobile, helping Kuli to grasp meaning straight away without lots of verbal explanation.

- By making most tasks or projects open-ended, ensuring that he learns the skills and processes along with the rest of the group, but then is allowed to develop his work in his own way (along with the rest of the group), Kuli will gain confidence in his own ability and he will see his efforts marked objectively without comparing like for like.

Harry (Dyslexia)

Harry is a very anxious child and although he has now started at secondary school, he still seems to be a 'little boy'. His parents have been very concerned about his slow progress in reading and writing and arranged for a dyslexia assessment when he was eight. They also employ a private tutor who comes to the house for two hours per week and they spend time each evening and at weekends hearing him read and working on phonics with him.

Harry expresses himself well orally, using words which are very sophisticated and adult. His reading is improving (RA 8.4) but his handwriting and spelling are so poor that it is sometimes difficult to work out what he has written. He doesn't just confuse *b* and *d* but also *h* and *y*, *p* and *b*. Increasingly, he uses a small bank of words that he knows he can spell.

Some staff get exasperated with Harry as he is quite clumsy, seems to be in a dream half the time and cannot remember a simple sequence of instructions. He has difficulty telling left from right and so is often talking about the wrong diagram in a book or out of step in PE and sport. 'He's just not trying,' said one teacher, while others think he needs 'to grow up a bit'.

He is popular with the girls in his class and recently has made friends with some of the boys in the choir. Music is Harry's great passion but his parents are not willing for him to learn an instrument at the moment.

Strategies

- Staff to talk to the parents about Harry's lack of confidence.

- Provide Harry with strategies for distinguishing left from right. Art teachers could take a lead in this, trying out what works best with Harry such as the use of symbols, colours, etc.

- Find out from parents/SENCO how he has learned things and see if similar strategies would work in the classroom.

- Investigate the possibility of using a computer with spellchecker at home and school to cope with orthographic and spelling difficulties.

- Offer lots of praise for all aspects of practical work.

- Art and design may be a subject in which Harry, if not already possessing confidence, can build confidence rapidly as the subject is not heavily reliant on the written word. Teachers can find other ways for him to record his feelings, the work of other artists etc. by exploiting his preferred learning style (Visual/Auditory/Kineasthetic) and by assisting with any annotations which are required.

- To address Harry's clumsiness, the teacher could differentiate by pace and set him one task per lesson to allow extra time to complete and achieve.

- Allow him to use materials that do not require fine use, such as oil or chalk pastels, clay for imprinting, and also allowing him to record his work using a digital camera to compile an e-sketchbook.

- It is vital that the teacher ensures he can see success in his work and abilities, even if his progress is limited.

Megan (Wheelchair user)

Everyone knows when Megan is around! She is very outgoing, loud and tough. Megan has spina bifida and needs a wheelchair and personal care as well as educational support. She has upset a number of the less experienced classroom assistants, who find her a real pain. Some of the teachers like her because she is very sparky. If she likes a subject, she works hard – or at least she did until this year.

Megan has to be up very early for her parents to help get her ready for school before the bus comes at 7.50 am. She lives out of town and is one of the first to be picked up and one of the last to be dropped off so she has a longer school day than many of her classmates. Tiredness can be a problem as everything takes her so long to do and involves so much effort.

Now she is 15, she has started working towards her GCSEs and has the potential to get several A to Cs particularly in maths and sciences. She is intelligent but is in danger of becoming disaffected because everything is so much harder for her than for other children. Recently she has lost her temper with a teacher, made cruel remarks to a very sensitive child and turned her wheelchair round so she sat with her back to a supply teacher. She has done no homework for the last few weeks saying that she doesn't see the point as 'no one takes a crip seriously.'

Strategies

- The school needs to identify staff she is on good terms with and make sure she spends time with people she respects.

- Urgent support is needed to minimise the physical effort involved in writing and recording.

- Staff need to discuss things with her instead of talking behind her back and give her some respect.

- The school needs to establish ground rules about behaviour.

- Consider cutting back on the number of subjects she is taking.

- Have higher expectations of her.

- Rotate Teaching Assistants so she doesn't wear them out.

- Talk to parents about her health – has there been some deterioration? Problems at home?

- Organise her art and design practical work carefully, so that practical difficulties do not prevent her achieving and presenting a piece of work that has real meaning for her personally.

- Allow as much independence as possible in setting her own projects within parameters of the skill and element tasks that are required to achieve the expected outcome.

Project Example for Megan: Blue Boxes (Mixed Media)

This project creates a 'box of ideas' based on the real and imagined. It allows Megan to explore a theme, to recreate a mood by the inclusion of a 'real object'. The Dada and Surrealist artist Duchamp and more recently Damien Hurst have explored the potential of everyday objects (the bicycle wheel, the shell and the urinal for example). A real object brings with it associated thoughts and ideas relevant to Megan's life and experiences. The box may be created developing the formal elements of colour, shape, pattern, texture, line and form.

The box therefore may include the following ideas:

- sketchpad with visual notes – a nearby river or sea or imagined environs or a still life with bucket and spade;
- driftwood and natural finds;
- message in a bottle;
- a collection of blue objects: buttons, tickets, wools and/or badges etc.;
- maps of seas: Pacific, Atlantic, Indian Ocean etc.;
- fishing tackle: nets, line, hook and float;
- toy boats and floating objects;
- words associated with travel and time;
- plaster casts of prints in the sand;
- postcards of sea artists such as Turner, Alfred Wallis, Christopher Wood and Ben Nicholson.

Picasso's Blue period may be a relevant discussion when examining the theme of 'blue'. Poverty, sadness, the sea and sky.

The 'box' allows Megan to develop techniques for paint, print, weaving, drawing, collage and photography. Alternately the work could be developed on a computer programme such as Photoshop and the resulting manipulated digital photographs mounted within a wooden box found at a greengrocer's, for example.

Artist for Blue Boxes: Joseph Cornell 1903–72

Joseph Cornell was an American artist. He sold refrigerators from door to door and came across collages by Ernst and works by other Surrealists at the Julien Levy Gallery in New York. He created his first collages and montages of old engravings and held his first one-man show at the Julien Levy Gallery. Working as a textile designer (1934–40), he collected old films and photographs and also bought objects, papers and early image, which he used in his 'boxes' and collages. Some of the elements Cornell included in his 'boxes' had autobiographical associations, derived in particular from his research into ballet, cinema and history, such as the tiny scenes in which he organised his maps of the night sky, clay pipes, rings, parrots and glass balls. These assemblages, like his collages, are both enigmatic and disturbing but without aggression. Cornell's work seems indifferent to a social dimension. His constructions reflect a personal meditation and a rare poetic richness.

Navigation Series Box (1950) in Musée de Grenoble is particularly apt when exploring a river or the sea and reflecting on the subject of 'Navigation'. For the young Key Stage 4 student, a 'Blue Box' entitled 'Navigating through Life' may be an appropriate starting point for a project.

Steven (Emotional, behavioural and social difficulties)

'Stevie' is a real charmer – sometimes! He is totally inconsistent: one day, he is full of enthusiasm, the next day, he is very tricky and he needs to be kept on target. He thrives on attention. In primary school, he spent a lot of time sitting by the teacher's desk and seemed to enjoy feeling special. If he sat there he would get on with his work, but then as soon as he moved to sit with his friends he wanted to make sure he was the centre of attention.

Now in Year 8, Steven sometimes seems lazy – looking for the easy way out – but at other times he is quite dynamic and has lots of bright ideas. He can't work independently and has a very short attention span. No one has very high expectations of him and he is not about to prove them wrong.

Some of the children don't like him because he can be a bully but really he is not nasty. He is a permanent lieutenant for some of the tougher boys and does things to win their approval.

He is a thief but mostly he takes silly things, designed to annoy rather than for any monetary value. He was found with someone's library ticket and stole one shoe from the changing rooms during PE.

Since his mother has begun a relationship with a new partner, there has been a deterioration in behaviour and Steven has also been cautioned by police after stealing from a local DIY store. He has just been suspended for throwing a chair at a teacher but, staff suspect, this was because he was on a dare. He certainly knows how to get attention.

Strategies

- Structured programme with lots of rewards – certificates, merits etc.

- Praise to overcome negative self-image.

- Success to build confidence.

- Information in short chunks.

- Lots of changes of activity.

- Give him some responsibility.

- Opportunities to design and make an object, for example a mask, that he feels he has ownership of.

- Positive support in the artroom that allows him to produce a satisfactory piece of work that he is proud of.

- Regular feedback and skill support to help him improve his work.

- Work in a supportive group that recognises his achievements in the art and design lessons.

Project example for Steven: The Green Man Key Stage 3 (3D and Print)

A project relating to mask making and printing is inspired by the green foliage of a local park. A Green Man can be seen as a misericord in cathedrals or as part of the mythology of the countryside.

The foliate head or leaf mask, from which the Green Man ultimately derives, appeared in Roman art during the second half of the first century. Male masks with acanthus scrolls sprouting from their faces were reproduced on friezes on both triumphal arches of Septimius Severus in Rome and on Aurelian's Temple of the Sun, also in Rome; the Green Man is probably the most common decorative motif of medieval sculpture that has been left to us. It can be found on roof bases, capitals, corbels, fonts, tombs, tympana, screens, bench ends, misericords and arm rests. The idea of a face in the leaves excites an imaginative response.

In Botticelli's 'Primavera' the rhythm of the picture is set in motion by the blue-green god of the west wind Zephyrus flying through the branches of a tree to embrace the nymph Chloris, whose name signifies 'green'. Out of her mouth pours the flowers – just like a Green Man – through which she is transformed into the goddess Flora.

Key works which explore the 'Green Man' theme include:
'Primavera' by Botticelli (1478)
The leaf sculptures of Andy Goldsworthy
The myth of Aphrodite and Adonisn – Adonis is born from a tree
The story of Robin Hood. He is the watcher through the leaves, the burst of laughter in an empty clearing, the joker in the ambush.
The story of Isis and Osiris from Ancient Egypt. Osiris was the corn, the vine and the trees: his mummy is sometimes shown sprouting with ears of wheat.

Resources

Photographs, reproductions, plant forms, a walk in a 'green environment', leaf collection, mask base, tissue paper, Modroc, paints, sketchbooks and drawing materials, glues, wools, polystyrene squares and water-based printing inks.

Learning outcomes

To design and develop a mask based on the theme of the Green Man using a papier mâché mask base built up over either a clay or plastic mould. Modroc, plaster impregnated bandage, is an alternative method. The masks can be painted/varnished and/or covered in tissue paper, home-made paper, twigs etc.

Green Man still life prints: a still life may be set up, plant forms, mask moulds, branches and bark. Prints may be developed from drawings of the shapes, patterns and forms found in the still life. Polystyrene squares, torn or straight, may be indented using a biro to create the designs; or using cardboard and paper, a relief print can be built up for 'mono-printing'.

Experiment and explore

Sketchpad experiments relating to the colour green in a variety of materials, paint, pastel, crayon, tissue paper etc. Still life observation drawings and paintings. Carnival mask research based on the premise that masks have a paradoxical use – they both conceal and transform. A masquerader is transformed by his/her mask into a new identity; the masker is now free to act according to his/her mask character.

Record

Observation drawings of leaves, masks and still life. Colour experiments of green. Details from 'Green Man' found in churches. Look at some of Henry Rousseau's jungle paintings and 'A Carnival Evening' and record appropriate details.

Develop

Discuss the designs experimented with and develop a mask and/or print based on the most appropriate ideas.

Evaluate work in progress

Discuss the effectiveness of chosen materials, designs, mask shapes and prints.

Represent

Discuss the idea of representing a mask by 'making-up' a face with face paints or theatrical make-up to produce paintings on the Green Man/Carnival/Self-Portraiture theme. Photographs of the pupils' faces may be used as a basis of the paintings.

Evaluate

Has this been an interesting project that may lead onto further developments, for example exploring the 'Carnival' theme? Has it taught visual and tactile elements, developing skills in drawing, print making, painting and colour mixing, designing and making sculpture? Has Stevie created art work that is relevant and possibly magical to him?

Artist for the Green Man project: Andy Goldsworthy

Horse chestnut leaves
sections torn out leaving the veins
stitched together with grass stalks
hung in the darkness of rhododendron and yew.

Andy Goldsworthy was born in 1956 in Cheshire. He grew up in Yorkshire, where he made his first outdoor sculptures. He works with stone, earth, snow, ice, wood, water, plant form and has increasingly broadened his working landscape by visiting remote areas of the world – the Arctic, Australian desert, Japan, the USA. His often ephemeral sculptures are photographically recorded.

Since his student days he has worked largely in the open air, using materials that he has found around him, displaying a sympathetic contact with the natural world. He works with the landscape instinctively.

There is a potent recurring form in nature which I have explored through working with bracken, snow, sand, leaves, grass, trees and earth. . . It is the 'ridge' of a mountain, the roof of a tree, a river finding its way down the valley.

Matthew (Cognitive and learning difficulties)

Matt is a very passive boy. He has no curiosity, no strong likes or dislikes. One teacher said, 'He's the sort of boy who says yes to everything to avoid further discussion but I sometimes wonder if he understands anything.'

Now in Year 9, he is quite a loner. He knows all the children and does not feel uncomfortable with them but is always on the margins. Often in class he sits and does nothing, just stares into space. He is no trouble and indeed if there is any kind of conflict, he absents himself or ignores it. No one knows very much about him as he never volunteers any information. In French, he once said that he had a dog and one teacher has seen him on the local common with a terrier, but no one is sure if it is his.

He does every piece of work as quickly as possible to get it over with. His work is messy and there is no substance to anything he does, which makes it hard for teachers to suggest a way forward, or indeed to find anything to praise. Matthew often looks a bit grubby and is usually untidy. He can be quite clumsy and loses things regularly but does not bother to look for them. He does less than the minimum.

He is in a low set for maths but stays in the middle. He has problems with most humanities subjects because he has no empathy and no real sense of what is required. When the class went to visit a museum for their work on the Civil War, he was completely unmoved. To him, it was just another building and he could not really link it with the work they had done in history.

Strategies

- Get parents/carers in to find out if he has any enthusiasms at home.

- Involve him in pair work with a livelier pupil who will gee him up a bit.

- Set up situations where he can make a contribution.

- Set up some one-to-one sessions with a TA where he is pushed to respond.

- Get him using technology to improve the appearance of his work, perhaps in a homework club after school.

- Break up the project into small achievable sections.

- Encourage Matthew to look at designs for mountain bicycles, skateboards or cars etc. and encourage him to collect or add to a collage of 'machines'.

- Give constant support when he is working within the group, giving him a supportive buddy to help design a tee-shirt, relating to the theme 'Man and Machine'.

Project example for Matthew: Man and Machine Key Stage 3 (Collage and Photographic Collage leading to a tee-shirt design)

The aim of this project is to explore the industrial world and its 'manufactured' image. There may be an opportunity to make an implicit social comment on the recycling of material waste.

Key works which explore this 'Machine Age' theme include:

'Car door, Ironing Board and Twin-Tub with North American Headdress' (1981), Bill Woodrow, Tate Gallery, Liverpool

'The Machine Minders' (1956), Ghisha Koenig, Modern British Art, Tate Gallery, Liverpool

'Workshop' (1914–15), Percy Wyndham Lewis, Modern British Art, Tate Gallery, Liverpool

'The City' (1919), Fernand Léger, Philadelphia Museum of Art

Paolozzis' work housed at the Dean Gallery, Edinburgh

Learning outcomes

A group of pupils, including Matthew, may develop a collage of 'factory' studies, employing a variety of materials to convey the world of the machine, including photo collage images. This class mural may also explore the theme of materials used in the built environment, brick, steel, iron, concrete, glass, stone, wood, aluminium and neoprene.

Experiment and explore

From a collection of machine pieces, e.g. engine parts, cogs, wheels, wires, old computer parts and bicycles, Matthew may create drawings using a variety of pens, pencils, chalk and charcoal or ICT.

Record

Miniature 'collaged' structures from a variety of materials such as plastic, corrugated card, straws, tin foil-covered shapes etc. to create a 'contemporary' factory. Photograph pipes, machines (including skateboards, mountain bicycles etc.), factory buildings and industrial waste.

Develop

Small paintings from a detail of the photographs or collage exploring a colour theme to match the factory process, e.g. blues/purples for a jeans factory, reds for a skateboard factory etc.

Evaluate work in progress

What developments, drawings, collages, photographs, paintings will combine most effectively to create the mural? Can computer images develop further ideas?

Represent 1

By pressing machine pieces into wet sand, pour in plaster and create Paolozzi-style structures. This more tactile workshop may encourage Matthew and a few chosen pupils to take this project into 3D. 'I want them to be works which will inspire an architect when he looks up from the drawing board.' (Eduardo Paolozzi)

Represent 2

Scan in the collage, painting or digital image of the plaster cast to produce a tee-shirt design which can be printed onto a tee-shirt using special printer paper (available from PC World, etc.) which should be flipped over so any wording is in reverse, and then once printed out this design can be ironed onto the tee-shirt. This may give Matthew a real sense of achievement and a sense of belonging to the group.

Evaluate

By discussing the effectiveness of the mural and the recycling of the materials used, pupils will be able to discuss the merits of a plastic, steel, wooden or stone building form and perhaps align this with environmental projects. Photographs of the mural produced with the tee-shirts being worn by the pupils and a display of made and collected man-made objects may help the pupils, including Matthew, assess their achievements.

Bhavini (Visual impairment)

Bhavini has very little useful sight. She uses a stick to get around school and some of the other children make cruel comments about this which she finds very hurtful. She also wears glasses with thick lenses which she hates. On more than one occasion, she has been knocked over in the corridor but she insists that these incidents were accidents and that she is not being bullied. However, her sight is so poor she may not recognise pupils who pick on her.

She has a certain amount of specialist equipment such as talking scales in food technology, a CCTV for textbooks, and now in Year 9, she is always conscious of being different. Her classmates accept her but she is very cut off as she does not make eye contact or see well enough to find people she knows to sit with at break. She spends a lot of time hanging around the support area. Her form tutor has tried to get other children to take her under their wing or to escort her to humanities, which is in another building, but this has bred resentment. She has friends outside school at the local Phab club (Physically handicapped/able bodied) and has taken part in regional VI Athletics tournaments, although she opts out of sport at school if she can. Some of the teachers are concerned about health and safety issues and there has been talk about her being disapplied from science.

She has a reading age approximately three years behind her chronological age and spells phonetically. Many of the teaching strategies used to make learning more interesting tend to disadvantage her. The lively layout of her French book with cartoons and speech bubbles is a nightmare. Even if she has a page on her CCTV or has a photocopy of the text enlarged she cannot track which bit goes where. At the end of one term she turned up at the support base asking for some work to do because 'they're all watching videos.'

Strategies

- Her isolation is the key factor and needs addressing most urgently.

- In the artroom, to help her feel a real sense of achievement she needs to work within a supportive group and if at all possible with a member of the support staff.

- The visual aids need to be bold, clear and colourful.

- Projects based in 3D allow tactile engagement and with appropriate support a sense of achievement in producing a ceramic container, papier mâché bowl etc.

Project example for Bhavini: Containers Key Stage 3 (3D)

This project may be developed from a visit to a local church, gallery, museum or multicultural centre, looking at the work of Christo or a chosen building, and then by exploring the theme of containers to include a variety of materials, ceramic, papier mâché bowls, wooden boxes, bottles, constructions and wrappings.

1   Ceramic slab pots or architectural-inspired containers relating to the built environment. Keynote artist Alison Britton. Bhavini may press small objects into the clay, e.g. shells, cogs, etc. to develop a design.

2   Papier mâché bowls developed from bold African/Aboriginal designs, ceramic details or architectural forms.

3   Wooden boxes or sets of drawers purchased from IKEA or similar stores or made in design technology lessons may be painted/decorated with designs based on the above themes.

4   Bottles painted in the style of Magritte. A surreal view of a local landscape or environment.

5   A 'home-made paper book' to reference ideas leading to the final project, using drawing materials and simple print techniques.

6   Explore the work of Aboriginal/African designs or Christo and Jean Claude and Magritte. These references have bold and colourful designs for Bhavini to research.

Artist for the container project: Christo and Jeanne-Claude

Christo: born in 1935, Christo Javacheff Gabrow, of a Bulgarian industrialist family. Jeanne-Claude: born Jeanne-Claude de Guillebou, in Casablanca, of a French military family. 1953-56: Christo studied at the Fine Arts Academy, Sofia, and then via Prague to study at the Vienna Fine Arts Academy. Arrived in Paris in 1958 and began 'wrapping' objects. By 1964, with their son, they had settled in New York permanently. In 1969 they embarked on the first of their large-scale projects: 'Wrapped Coast', a rocky Australian coast 'wrapped' in white cloth that folded and unfolded with the tide.

In 1995 they wrapped the Reichstag in Berlin. Like Schinkel's extravagant, elaborate and theatrical design for a monument to Frederick the Great, the 'Wrapped Reichstag' has with time become almost a legend.

Today the Reichstag is full of details, very broken, all these little ornaments and fragments, and when it is wrapped the fabric will really create a new form. There will be only the fabric to give a completely new form – the folds of silver fabric cascading from the top like water, highlighting the many points that cannot be seen today in the real architecture.

The fabric will be off the wall – one or two metres off – allowing the cloth to breathe and to give thus constant motion unlike normal architecture of very sturdy materials; the material will be always moving with the wind. It will not disturb the use of the building, people can go in and out. It will be like a curtain, and perfectly airy. (Christo)

The fabric used was real aluminium powder electrified on the surface; real metal gives this enormously rich quality.

Christo's work is 'ephemeral' and the only recorded results of the culmination of such a long-term planning operation are photographs and drawings in pencil, charcoal, crayon, pastel and technical data. His ideas are uncomfortably avant-garde but over three million people were lured to view the wrapped Pont Neuf in Paris.

Christo and Jean-Claude drape, colour and transform places or structures rather like painters and sculptors, accentuating forms, highlighting aspects that are usually overlooked and suggesting new spatial relationships. Their works are like major construction projects, requiring the collaboration of administrators, industrialists and a large workforce.

Ideas for 'Containers'

The act of placing something in a container: for storage, safe keeping, transport, a secret hiding place, e.g. message in a bottle, envelopes and postcards, smuggler's box, jewellery box. . . e.g. environment in a box, memory box, matchbox project, placing objects in a bottle, sending something through the post. . .

Man-made containers: Bags, boxes, jars, vases, bottles . . . construction, materials, form of decoration, fastenings. . .

The surprise element of opening a container: unwrapping a Christmas present, jack-in-a-box, snake boxes, box within a box, Russian dolls, puzzle pots, spider in a matchbox. . .

Natural containers: Shells, seedpods, chrysalis, skins. . . Construction, form, shape, pattern, texture, colour. . .

Susan (Complex difficulties, Asperger's Syndrome)

Susan is a tall, very attractive girl who has been variously labelled as having Asperger's and 'cocktail party syndrome'. She talks fluently but usually about something totally irrelevant. She is very charming and her language is sometimes quite sophisticated but her ability to use language for school work in Year 10 operates at a much lower level. Her reading is excellent on some levels but she cannot draw inferences from the printed word. If you ask her questions about what she has read, she looks blank, echoes what you have said, looks puzzled or changes the subject – something she is very good at.

She finds relationships quite difficult. She is very popular, especially with the boys in her class. They think she is a laugh. There have been one or two problems with some of the boys in her school. Her habit of standing too close to people and her over-familiarity have led to misunderstandings which have upset her. Her best friend Laura is very protective of her and tries to mother her, to the extent of doing some of her work for her so she won't get into trouble.

Her work is limited. In art, all her pictures look the same, very small cramped drawings and she does not like to use paint because it is 'messy'. She finds it very hard to relate to the wider world and sees everything in terms of her own experience. The class have been studying *Macbeth* and she has not moved beyond saying, 'I don't believe in witches and ghosts'.

Some teachers think she is being wilfully stupid or not paying attention. She seems to be attention-seeking as she is very poor at turn taking and shouts out in class if she thinks of something to say or wants to know how to spell a word. When she was younger, she used to retreat under the desk when she was upset and had to be coaxed out. She is still easily offended and cannot bear being teased. She has an answer for everything and while it may not be sensible or reasonable, there is an underlying logic.

Strategies

- To help her become more independent – try using computer software in art lessons in the first instance, which is not 'messy', in order for Susan to achieve in a different medium. Animation packages such as 'Kar2ouche' (Immersive Education) allow the manipulation of given images which will help to build confidence, but students can combine these with their own drawings or designs, given or recorded sounds, which make the whole experience more personal. There is *Kar2ouche* software on Macbeth (one of many titles in many subject areas) which may help Susan in her English lessons also.

- To count to 20 before shouting out – when teaching the whole class, allow thinking time for responses that is, in most cases, longer than 8 seconds (which feels like a long time!) so that all students are required to think before responding – again, not making Susan's 'counting' time so obvious.

- Move her away from Laura – perhaps next to another female student whose drawing skills aren't as developed as Susan's and encourage occasional peer tutoring.

- Writing frames and examples of past students' work that she can model her responses on.

- Discussion of social issues, body language, appropriate behaviour, etc – for example, this can be done in a Unit of Work via critical analysis of work by artists, sculptors, designers and makers which prompt discussion and provoke thought, such as the work of Cindy Sherman. This can also incorporate aspects of Susan's own experience in the artwork subsequently produced.

- Promote experimentation in lessons, especially in sketchbooks, gradually increasing scale, new materials and techniques, but allowing time for Susan to continue with small-scale drawings if she wishes.

Jenny (Down's Syndrome)

Jenny is in Year 7 and has Down's Syndome. She is a very confident child who has been cherished and encouraged by her mother and older brothers and sisters. She is very assertive and is more than capable of dealing with spiteful comments: 'I don't like it when you call me names. You're cruel and I hate you', but this assertiveness can lead to obstinacy. She is prone to telling teachers that they are wrong!

She has average skills in reading and writing but her work tends to be unimaginative and pedestrian. She enjoys biology but finds the rest of the science curriculum hard going. She has started to put on weight and tries to avoid PE. She has persuaded her mother to provide a note saying that she tires easily but staff know that she is a bundle of energy and is an active member of an amateur theatre group which performs musicals. She has a good singing voice and enjoys dancing.

She went to a local nursery and primary school and fitted in well. She always had someone to sit next to and was invited to all the best birthday parties. Teachers and other parents frequently praised her and she felt special.

Now in secondary school, everything has changed. Some of her friends from primary school have made new friendships and don't want to spend so much time with her. She is very hurt by this and feels excluded. She is also struck by how glamorous some of the older girls look and this has made her more self-conscious.

Strategies

- Talk to Jenny's parents about diet and exercise and find a way of making her feel more attractive.

- Encourage new groupings in class so she gets to meet other children from different feeder schools.

- Pair her up with a child who has better imaginative/empathy skills but weaker literacy so they can support each other.

- Use plenty of praise for her behaviour when it is good and positive feedback on her practical work, safe use of tools and materials, etc.

- Highlight and praise her contributions to group discussions that are based around a work of art. Use images that depict flights of fancy or wild imagination and which may spark a train of thought that Jenny can take into her own work as a starting point.

CHAPTER 7

Monitoring and Assessment

Pupils need to be assured that their successes will be recognised and rewarded and that, when they have difficulty accessing learning, the necessary support will be available. Teachers need to know when things are going well and when they are not, so that they can change their teaching approaches as appropriate (*SEN: Training Materials for the Foundation Subjects*, Introduction, DfES 2003).

The materials included in this book will support teachers in planning appropriate learning and assessment opportunities. They do not represent a separate curriculum for pupils with learning difficulties but run parallel to National Curriculum mainstream requirements. They demonstrate a process for developing access to the National Curriculum and support teachers in adapting and developing their own planning in order to respond to the needs of their pupils. Schools may already have effective structures but may wish to consider some of the exemplar materials and proformas for monitoring and assessment that are featured on the following pages and on the accompanying CD.

Individual Education Plans

IEPs are a useful tool in providing structured support in clear ways that allow the teacher to see at a glance any difficulties the pupil may have. Target-setting should involve the pupil and targets should be meaningful in order for them to fully understand what will improve their learning. They should not be as broad as 'work harder' but should be specific to extend progression of skills in art, craft and design. They should also highlight any additional or different support for the pupil with SEN that other mainstream pupils do not receive. Above all, it is important that any goals set are achievable and in this way motivation and self-esteem can be raised. (See the CD for how to make targets SMART and for an example of an IEP with art-specific targets.)

INDIVIDUAL EDUCATION PLAN

Name: Kelly	**Area of concern:** Dyslexia/SpLD
Year: 8	**Strengths:** Art and design work.
Stage:	
	Start date:
	Review date:
	IEP no.: 2

Targets:

- To understand the formal elements of art and design, for example line, colour, shape, tone, etc. relating these to specific projects.
- To use mind maps for recording and research artists.
- To bring sketchbook, pencils and required materials for the art lesson.

Strategies for use in class:

- Provide key subject/project word lists.
- Encourage alternative methods of recording, e.g. sketches, collage, mind maps.
- Give differentiated homework sheets to match the project being followed in class.
- Give her extra time for tasks.
- Praise for experimentation and enthusiasm; exciting sketchpad.

Teacher/support:

Role of parent(s)/carer(s):

- Encourage with organisation and homework – list on kitchen noticeboard.
- Support research work for art lessons such as going out sketching, collecting materials, research on the Internet, etc.

Success criteria:

- Can use the formal elements of art and design when discussing, for example, a landscape project.
- Can use a sketchpad confidently.
- Is proud of her developing portfolio.

Resources:

- Prompt cards, word lists or displays as mobiles and/or in sketchpads of the formal elements.
- Examples on display of good sketchbook work.
- Visual reminder for project outcomes.
- Highlight homework tasks on sheet.
- Tick sheet for teachers to record whether she has completed the homework and project development.

Agreed by:

SENCO:

Parent(s)/carer(s):

Pupil:

Date:

Examples of Planning Sheets

Department of Art and Design: Planning for Key Stage 3

Year Group	Themes	Processes	Textiles	Printmaking	3D Studies
7	Portraiture/landscape/ manmade & natural forms	Mark making, materials, colour, form, space, texture, pattern	Weaving, tie dye, applique, transfer print (fabric crayon)	Monoprinting	Papier mâché, found materials, cane
8	Plants & animals/performing arts/cultural identity	As above but becoming more accurate and expressive with emphasis on more sensitive observation drawings	Batik, silk painting, screen printing	Basic relief printing e.g. pressprint	As above but in a more exploratory and developmental way. Modroc, modelling wire.
9	Human figure/containers/ architecture	Use of a wide range of materials in a thoughtful and experimental way	Above skills used in a more refined way as part of a design process, hand and machine stitching	Lino printing, screen printing	Papier mâché, found materials, chicken wire and Modroc

Department of Art and Design Long-Term Planning: Key Stage 3 Schemes of Work

	Year 7 Date:	Year 8 Date:	Year 9 Date:
Projects covered:			
Drawing from observation:			
Processes, activities and outcomes:			
Critical studies:			
Focus for assessment:			

WHAT THE UNITS COVER:

Art	Craft	Design	2D	3D	Shape	Form
Line	Tone	Colour	Pattern	Texture	Textiles	Space
Painting	Collage	Print-making	Digital media	Sculpture	Individual work	Collaborative work

Art Medium-Term Planning: Key Stage 3

THEME/TOPIC: African Art	YEAR GROUP: 8	CLASS: EK	TERM: Aut.	TIME ALLOCATION: 1 term

PROJECT OUTLINE:

Pupils will study African art through masks, sculptures and pattern work. Pupils will learn the technique of scraffito using oil pastels, Indian black ink and scraper tools. From observation of an African mask, pupils will produce a composition which will include African patterns in the background. Pupils will then transfer their drawing into a design for a 3D mask which will be made from cardboard and paint.

CURRICULAR LINKS

- PHSE
- History
- Geography
- Citizenship
- Textiles

KEY VOCABULARY

- African art
- Mask
- Pattern
- Decoration
- Scraffito
- Colour
- Mark making
- Transfer

LEARNING OBJECTIVES

- To learn the technique of scraffito using oil pastels and black ink.
- To have a greater understanding of pattern, colour, texture and decoration in African art.
- To have a greater understanding of the use of masks in African culture.
- To produce a drawing of African masks combined with pattern using African art and textiles for inspiration.
- To produce a three-dimensional mask from card and paint.

LEARNING OUTCOMES

Expectations at the end of this unit will be:

- A scraffito drawing of an African mask using oil pastels and ink surrounded by African patterns.
- A 3D African mask made from card and paint.

ASSESSMENT OPPORTUNITIES

- Ability to produce a drawing in class from observation of an African mask.
- Ability to develop an awareness of pattern, colour and design.
- Homework tasks to include research of African patterns.
- Ability to produce a composition of African masks and patterns and successfully transfer a design to card and paint.

MATERIALS/RESOURCES:

Paper
Pencils
Oil pastels
Reproductions of African masks and patterns
Black Indian ink
Card
Scissors, knives and cutting board
Coloured paint

LEVEL 4/5/6

HEALTH AND SAFETY: In addition to normal health and safety policy:
- Use of scraper blades for scraffito
- Use of craft knives and scissors to cut out card

DIFFERENTIATION:
- Outcome and success of mask scraffito drawing
- Interpretation of African patterns
- Design and detail of mask design
- Individual help and support given during lesson time

CONTEXT	KEY SKILLS	OPPORTUNITIES	STIMULUS	SUBJECTS SKILLS	CREATIVE PROCESS	ELEMENTS	ORGANISATION
Spiritual	Communication	Exploring and developing ideas	Art/craft/design	Drawing	Exploration	Line	Individual
Moral	Application of number	Investigating and making	People	Painting	Observation	Tone	Group
Social	ICT	Evaluating and developing work	Places	Printmaking	Imagination	Colour	Whole class
Cultural	Working with others	Knowledge and understanding	Objects	Modelling	Memory	Shape	Scale
Environmental	Improving own learning		Western	Constructing	Expression	Pattern	Sketchbooks
			Non-Western	Collage	Illustration	2D/3D	Display
			Historical	Textiles	Texture	Techniques/skills	
			Contemporary	ICT	Design	Form	
			Galleries/museums	Mixed Media	Critical studies	Space	

Teacher Assessment Proforma	
Name	**Form 9**

ART AND DESIGN

(A–G)	(1–4)	
Attainment ☐	**Effort** ☐	**Homework** ☐
	Conduct ☐	**Presentation** ☐

Knowledge and understanding of critical studies. ☐

Understanding and use of a variety of materials, tools and techniques. ☐

Key Stage 3 Teacher Assessment

During Key Stage 3 pupils develop their creativity and imagination through more sustained activities. These help them to build on and improve their practical and critical skills and to extend their knowledge and experience of materials, processes and practices. They engage confidently with art, craft and design in the contemporary world and from different times and cultures. They become more independent in using the visual language to communicate their own ideas, feelings and meanings.

At the end of each key stage, pupils are awarded a level of attainment between 1 and 8. The expected attainment for the majority of pupils at the end of KS3 is level 5 or 6.

Based on ongoing assessment and an end of KS3 assignment:

Level reached at end of KS3 ☐

Teacher Comment:
Signed

Level descriptors

P-levels have been devised for pupils with special needs who are not yet working at a level commensurate with National Curriculum level 1. They are now being widely used in special schools, and increasingly in mainstream schools as a way of recording even the smallest amounts of progress. The early levels 1–3 are generic and levels 4–8 are specific to art and design, as outlined below.

Performance descriptions in art and design

From level P4 to P8, it is possible to describe pupils' performance in a way that indicates the emergence of skills, knowledge and understanding in art and design. The descriptions provide an example of how this can be done.

P4 Pupils show some awareness of cause and effect in a creative process. They explore materials systematically, for example, tearing and scrunching paper to complete a collage. They are aware of starting or stopping a process. They make marks intentionally on a surface with fingers or tools, for example, pressing objects into clay or putting paint on paper. They repeat an activity to make the same or similar effect. They show an active interest in a range of tools and materials, taking part in familiar activities with some support.

P5 Pupils handle or use tools and materials purposefully. They show preferences for activities and begin to carry out simple processes. They choose tools and materials which are appropriate to the activity, for example, picking brushes or rollers for painting. They show they can create and apply familiar techniques to a task, for example, manipulating and shaping malleable materials to produce a desired effect or applying glue to a surface to make materials stick together in making a model.

P6 Pupils show an intention to create. They start to use tools, materials and simple actions to produce a piece of work. They imitate the use of tools, materials and simple actions, for example, cutting. They practise new skills with less support, developing their knowledge of the process of making, for example, selecting and gathering suitable resources and tools for a piece of work.

P7 Pupils communicate ideas, events or experiences through their use of colour, form, line and tone. Working in two or three dimensions they may intentionally represent or symbolise an object or an emotion. They purposefully choose colours or techniques. They show confidence in using a variety of processes and make appropriate use of tools and materials.

P8 Pupils develop their ideas and use materials and processes working in two and three dimensions. They finish a piece of work following an established pattern of activity, for example, gathering appropriate materials, taking part in an activity and stopping work when finished. They know that paintings, sculptures and drawings have meaning. They use a growing art vocabulary and begin to express meaning in their own work.

When assessing pupil progress against level descriptors, it is advisable to take into consideration as many factors or examples of evidence as possible – even by making notes during group discussions. Reward pupils for their thinking and any aspect of practical art skill and explain next steps thoroughly to make goals more achievable.

Bibliography

The following books, artist references and artworks may be useful and are placed under the headings of the projects described in Chapter 5 and in the case studies in Chapter 6.

Project 1 The Iron Man

Anthony Gormley	*Critical Mass*	ISBN 0900946709
Elizabeth Frink	*Sculpture*	ISBN 0946425051
Giacometti	*Royal Academy London*	ISBN 7809035986
The Iron Man	*Ted Hughes*	ISBN 0571141498
Joseph Beuys		ISBN 1854375857

Artworks

Elizabeth Frink	Anglican Cathedral, Liverpool
Giacometti	Tate Liverpool and Tate Modern
Anthony Gormley	Yorkshire Sculpture Park, Bretton, Yorkshire

Project 2 Forms in a Landscape

Andy Goldsworthy	*Andy Goldsworthy*	ISBN 0670832138
BBC	*Working with contemporary art* (Video)	ISBN 0563463090
BBC	*Working with contemporary art* (Resource pack)	ISBN 0563463031
George Bain	*Celtic Art*	ISBN 0094618305
Michael Brennand-Wood	*Contemporary International Basketmaking*	ISBN 1858940788
Moorish Architecture		ISBN 3822896322

Artworks

Andy Goldsworthy	Yorkshire Sculpture Park Archives Royal Academy, London
Michael Brennand-Wood	Whitworth Art Gallery, Manchester Crafts Council, Islington www.Crafts Council.org.uk
Vincent Van Gogh	Arles, 'View from the Wheat Fields' (1888) Van Gogh Museum, Amsterdam
William Morris	Whitworth Art Gallery

Project 3 Picasso, Plates and Portraiture

Lady Lever Art Gallery	*Guide to the Lady Lever Art Gallery*	ISBN 0901534943
Michael Sandle	*Memorials for the Twentieth Century*	ISBN 1854371665
Pablo Picasso	*First Discovery*	ISBN 185103255X
Marilyn McCully (ed.)	*Picasso: Painter and Sculptor in Clay*	ISBN 0900946636

Artworks

Julia Carter Preston	Bluecoat Display Centre, Walker Art Gallery, Liverpool
	Lady Lever Art Gallery, Port Sunlight, Wirral
Picasso Ceramics	Musée Picasso, Antibes
Picasso Ceramics	Royal Academy, London
Picasso Ceramics	Musée Picasso, Paris

Project 4 Identity

Looking at Pictures: An Introduction to Art for Young People	ISBN 0713646853
Masquerade	ISBN 0953132900
Picture Poems	ISBN 0340679875
The National Gallery Collection	ISBN 0947645060
Voices in the Gallery Poems and Pictures	ISBN 0946590540
With a Poets Eye	ISBN 0946590389

Artworks: Portraiture

Drumcroon Arts Education Centre, Wigan
Lady Lever Art Gallery, Port Sunlight, Wirral
National Gallery, London
National Portrait Gallery, London and Edinburgh
Tate Modern/Britain/Liverpool and St Ives

Artworks: Masks

British Museum, London
The Museum of Mankind, London
The Victoria and Albert Museum, London
The Gordon Reece Gallery, 16 Cufford Street, London

The video work of Bill Viola (a catalogue of his work) is available from The National Gallery in London.

Project 5 Flight

Elizabeth Frink	*Sculpture*	ISBN 0946425051
Anthony Gormley	*Critical Mass*	ISBN 0900946709
David Hill	*Turner's Birds*	ISBN 0714825328
The National Gallery Collection		ISBN 0947645160
Thames & Hudson	*Art 20th Century CD-ROM*	ISBN 0500100152
Michael & Peter Benton	*Picture Poems*	ISBN 0340879875
	Voices in a Gallery	ISBN 0946590540

Artworks

Audubon	Liverpool University Gallery
Albrecht Dürer	National Gallery, London
Elizabeth Frink	Liverpool Cathedral
Anthony Gormley	The Angel of the North
Fredrick Leighton	WalkerArt Gallery, Liverpool
Nike of Samothrace	Louvre Gallery, Paris
JMW Turner	The Tate Britain
Leonardo da Vinci	National Gallery, London

Project 6 Water

Noel G. Smith	*Almost an Island*	ISBN 0951776207
Michael & Peter Benton	*Picture Poems*	ISBN 0340679875
Matthew Gale	*Alfred Wallis*	ISBN 1854372289
David Hockney	*You Make the Picture*	ISBN 0901673528

Artworks

David Hockney	*Geometric Waves (1989)*	Private Collection of the Artist
David Hockney		Tate Modern, London Bradford Art Galleries & Museums
Hokusai	*The Great Wave (1931)*	Victoria & Albert Museum, London
Picasso	*The Bathers (1918)*	Musée Picasso, Paris
Turner	*Rough Sea (1840)*	Clore Gallery, Tate Britain, London
Turner	*Venice (1840)*	Walker Art Gallery, Liverpool

Alfred Wallis	*The Blue Ship (1934)*	Tate Gallery, St Ives
Catalogue 2001	*At Sea*	Tate Gallery, Liverpool

Case study example projects

Blue Boxes

Norbert Lynton	*The Story of Modern Art*	ISBN 0714818488
Thames & Hudson	*Multi Media Dictionary of Modern Art*	CD-ROM
Tate Gallery Liverpool	*Working with Modern British Art*	

Artworks

Joseph Cornell	*Navigation Series Box (1950)*	Musée de Grenoble
Marcel Duchamp	*Fountain (1917)*	Sidney Janis Gallery, New York
Damien Hurst Forms	*Without Life (1991)*	Tate Gallery, Liverpool
Christopher Wood	*Boat in Harbour, Brittany (1929)*	Tate Gallery, St Ives

The Green Man

Andy Goldsworthy	*Andy Goldsworthy*	ISBN 0670832138
Kathleen Basford	*The Green Man*	ISBN 0859914976
William Anderson	*Green Man*	ISBN 0005992524

Artworks

Henri Rousseau	Tate Britain
Botticelli	Uffizzi Gallery, Florence
Elizabeth Frink	Tate Modern, London
Andy Goldsworthy	Yorkshire Sculpture Park

Man and Machine

Royal Academy of Arts	*Eduardo Paolozzi Pop Art (1991)*	ISBN 0297831127
Thames & Hudson	*Multi-media Dictionary of Modern Art*	(CD-ROM)
Tate Liverpool	*Working with Modern British Art: A Guide for Teachers*	
Dean Gallery, Edinburgh	*Eduardo Paolozzi*	

Artworks

Richard Deacon	*What Could Make Me Feel This Way (1993)*	Tate Gallery, Liverpool
Ghisha Koenig	*The Machine Minders (1956)*	Tate Gallery, Liverpool
Fernand Léger	*The City (1919)*	Philadelphia Museum of Art
Bill Woodrow	*Car door, ironing board etc. (1981)*	Tate Gallery, Liverpool
Percy Wyndham	*Workshop (1914–15)*	Tate Gallery, Liverpool

Containers

Decorated Skin		ISBN 0500283281
Taschen	*Christo and Jeanne-Claude 30 Postcards*	ISBN 3822892610
Hayward Gallery	*Magritte Catalogue 1994*	
Thames & Hudson	*Multi-Media Dictionary of Modern Art CD-ROM*	

Artworks

Alison Britton ceramics		Victoria and Albert Museum, London
Christo	*Wrapped Reichstag*	Collection Jean-Claude Christo, New York
Example of papier mâché containers		V&A Museum, London Crafts Council Gallery, London
Greek artefacts		British Museum, London
Julian Opie	*Imagine You Can Order These (1993)*	Lisson Gallery, London
Magritte bottle designs		Museum of Modern Art, Brussels

Resources

Websites

www.moma.org

www.artmuseum.net

www.theartgallery.com.au

www.museumfortextiles.on.ca

www.princetonol.com/groups/iad

www.artlex.com/ArtLex/collage.html

www.sdc.org.uk/museum/mus.html

www.philaprintshop.com/diction.html

www.metmuseum.org

www.impressionism.org

www.mcs.csuhayward.edu/˜malek/Surrealism/

www.amn.org

www.abstractart.20m.com

www.artofeurope.com

www.artincontext.org

www.arts.ufl.edu/art/rt_room

www.nga.gov

www.picasso.com

www.magixl.com

www.reliefshading.com

www.olejarz.com

www.getty.edu/artsednet

www.tate.org.uk/learning/learnonline

www.modernpainters.co.uk

www.craftscouncil.org.uk

www.nationalgallery.org.uk

www.drumcroon.org.uk

www.nsead.org

www.schoolzone.co.uk

www.learnevaluations.co.uk

Equipment

Art Pad

Selwyn Electronics, Chaucer Business Park, Kemsing, Sevenoaks, Kent TN15 6QY
www.selwyn.co.uk
connect@selwyn.co.uk

B Squared

Burnhill Business Park, Provident House, Burrell Row, High Street, Beckenham,
Kent BR3 1AT
[020 8249 6333]
www.bsquaredsen.co.uk
info@bsquaredsen.co.uk

B Squared produces useful record sheets which can be used to show small steps
of progress within the Art Curriculum and provide possible targets for IEPs. Two
sets of records cover the P levels and NC levels 1–5.

Appendices

Individual achievement sheet (P2)

B

B Squared

Name

Started .... Completed ....

Exploring and Developing Ideas	Investigating and Making Art, Craft and Design	Evaluating and Developing Work
☐ Works with an adult in order to explore materials	☐ Opportunity to observe a range of objects all the same colour	☐ Indicates preference for material
☐ Manipulates object	☐ With assistance puts objects of the same colour together	☐ Indicates preference for texture
☐ Turns object in hands	☐ Plays with wet and dry sand	☐ Indicates preference for pattern
☐ Examines material handed to them	☐ Plays with water	☐ Has a favourite puppet or object and shows pleasure when it appears
☐ Smells materials	☐ Runs hand through water	☐ Shows preference for certain images
☐ Rubs hands across surfaces	☐ Runs hand through liquids	☐ Responds to results of own action
☐ Handles a range of natural materials	☐ Runs hand through sand	☐ With assistance uses a paintbrush
☐ Handles a range of man-made materials	☐ Runs hand through loose substance e.g. rice	☐
☐	☐ Makes light patterns on a wall with a torch	
	☐ With some assistance manipulates modelling material	

Knowledge and Understanding

☐ Shows an awareness of the purpose of some objects	☐	☐
☐ Shows some recognition of tools' purpose	☐	☐
☐ Remembers for short period purpose of activity	☐	☐
☐ Holds object with palmer grip	☐	☐
☐ Turns head to follow light pattern		
☐	☐	☐

P2 (ii) Pupils begin to be proactive in their interactions. They communicate consistent preferences and affective responses, *for example, reaching for glittery materials in preference to others*. They recognise familiar people, events and objects, *for example, grasping a painting sponge*. They perform actions, often by trial and improvement.

Dates	Notes

© B Squared 2003 (reproduced with permission)

Individual achievement sheet (NC3)

B

B Squared

Name

Started .... Completed ....

Exploring and Developing Ideas	Investigating and Making Art, Craft and Design	Evaluating and Developing Work
☐ Makes thoughtful observations about starting point	☐ Begins to use line and shape to communicate ideas	☐ Modifies work while in progress
☐ Collects visual material to assist in development	☐ Begins to use colour and tone to communicate ideas	☐ Describes methods used and how they may be developed and adapted
☐ Compares the ideas and methods used by others	☐ Records images and ideas from first hand observation	☐ Considers views and suggestions from others about their work
☐ Considers why a piece of work is displayed in a position	☐ Draws what they see rather than what they know	☐ Adapts their work taking into account the views of others
☐ Considers the designs of specific site sculptures	☐ Creates a sequence to illustrate an event or issue	☐ Identifies the focal point of the picture
☐ Experiments with line and shape using a range of media	☐ With assistance drafts their work	☐ Evaluates the composition of their picture
☐ Identifies a range of shapes, patterns and textures of a building	☐ Combines and organises colour, shapes, pattern and texture using mixed media	☐ Knows when their work is complete
☐ Shows some awareness of scale	☐ Applies experiences of processes	☐ Compares the approaches in their own and others' work and evaluates
☐ Experiments with painting techniques	☐ Applies their experience of materials	☐ Suggests how the work should be displayed
☐ Explores the use of light and dark	☐ Explores the use of line to create pattern	☐ Seeks advice
☐ Uses a view finder to identify boundaries of picture	☐ Uses different types of line and tone in their work	☐
☐ Uses scrapbook to assist development of work	☐ Uses overlapping and size to create an illusion of depth	☐
☐ Makes notes along with their sketches in the sketchbook	☐ Draws from memory	☐
☐ Looks at design and style of familiar objects with historical and cultural influences	☐ Works collaboratively	☐
☐ Considers designs from a range of cultures	☐ Uses light and shadow in their work	
☐ Considers the purpose and design of familiar object	☐	
☐ Considers the work of the illustrator		
☐ Explores the idea of place		

(p.t.o.)

(Continued from previous page)

Exploring and Developing Ideas	Investigating and Making Art, Craft and Design	Evaluating and Developing Work
Knowledge and Understanding		
☐ Identifies the purpose ☐ Distinguishes foreground and background ☐ Identifies the focal point of a piece of work ☐ Recognises architecture as an art form ☐ Is familiar with the work of some famous artists ☐ Is aware that art styles change over time	☐ Distinguishes between drawing from observation and drawing from imagination ☐ Identifies the light source in artwork ☐ Recognises that many cultures use art in celebrations, rituals and festivals ☐ Knows how common art materials are used in art and design ☐ Aware that the horizon line is not always visible	☐ Knows where to locate reference material ☐ Identifies the principal types of painting, i.e. water and oil ☐ Identifies common crafts ☐ ☐

NC Level 3 Pupils explore ideas and collect visual and other information for their work. They investigate visual and tactile qualities in materials and processes, communicate their ideas and meanings, and design and make images and artefacts for different purposes. They comment on similarities and differences between their own and others' work, and adapt and improve their own.

Writing frame

Title of art work...

Background information

Who made the image or artefact? Where does it come from? What tradition does it belong to?

The artist or designer who made this piece is . . .

He/she lives and works in . . .

It comes from the tradition of . . . (European painting/aboriginal art/Chinese ceramics. . .)

What can you see?

What is it made from? Is the image realistic or abstract?

In the picture/sculpture I can see . . .

The piece is constructed from . . . /painted in . . . /drawn in . . .

Meaning

What do you think it is about? Does it have a story?

The picture/sculpture/photograph makes me think of . . .

I think the artist/photographer means to say that . . .

How has it been made up? What materials and processes have been used?

Texture, shape, form, space, line, tone and colour, composition, objects and symbols
Materials: natural, made, ephemeral, precious
Processes: painting, drawing, printmaking, sculpture, digital media

This piece is made out of . . .

The artist has used . . .

Materials are used to create a powerful effect by . . .

The use of . . . . makes us feel . . . .

What do you think of it?

What do you like/not like about it? Why?

I chose to write about this piece because . . .

What I particularly like about this piece is . . .

This is because . . .

What works well in this piece is the . . .

I like everything in this piece except . . .

This is because . . .

I have been inspired by this work to experiment with . . .

I would like to ask the maker:

(why they chose . . . /what they were thinking about when . . . /who inspired them)

Blank sequence for teaching writing

Establish clear aims	
Provide examples	
Explore the features of the text	
Define the conventions	
Demonstrate how it is written	
Compose together	
Scaffold the first attempts	
Independent writing	
Draw out key learning	

Key art words

Key Art Words

Portraiture
Identity, image, portray, portraiture, self-portrait, self-image, self-identity, personality, likeness, icon, character, memorabilia, popular culture.

Landscape
Sense of place, landscape, change, environment, native, colour, texture, light, atmosphere, mood, sensuous, natural forms.

Culture
Masks, masquerade, costume, culture, tradition, humour, celebration, weather, people, sketchbook, diary, museum.

The City
Cities, architecture, buildings, shape, form, space, colour, noise, bustle, people, movement, grids, structures, street furniture, pollution, metropolis, landmarks, atmosphere.

Ideas
First impressions, observe, analyse, describe, discuss, design, evaluate, imagine.

Drawing
Drawing, sketching, sketchbooks, media, materials, process, sculpture, wire, ink, pastel, charcoal, line, paint, textiles, illustration, design, observation, poster, nature, life, digital imaging.

Recycling
Recycling, environment, ordinary, everyday, scale, purpose, waste, treasure, beauty, domestic, fantastic, materials, sculpture, found objects, ready-made, rubbish, redundant, collections.

(See CD for this and individual key word lists.)

Year 7 questionnaire: Art and Design

Name: . . . . Form: . . . .

This questionnaire is simply to allow your teacher to find out how much you know about art and design and how much you have learned in your previous school. THIS IS NOT A TEST so do not panic. Please answer the questions honestly and without asking the person sitting next to you. We would like a true picture of your knowledge and understanding.

● Briefly explain what you think is meant by the following words:

LINE . . . .

TONE . . . .

FORM . . . .

TEXTURE . . . .

PATTERN . . . .

COLOUR . . . .

COMPOSITION . . . .

PERSPECTIVE . . . .

PORTRAIT . . . .

LANDSCAPE . . . .

STILL LIFE . . . .

● Do you know a famous artist who paints the following things?

PORTRAITS . . . .

LANDSCAPES . . . .

STILL LIFE . . . .

● Make a list of any other famous artists that you know about.

. . . .

. . . .

. . . .

● Tell us about your favourite art project that you did in your last school.

. . . .

. . . .

. . . .

● What are the three primary colours?

. . . .

- Have you been to any art galleries and if so which ones?

. . . .

- Name some things that you have drawn from observation and the kinds of materials that you have used.

. . . .

. . . .

. . . .

- Do you know any artists who are working today, i.e. CONTEMPORARY ARTISTS?

. . . .

. . . .

- Have you ever used a computer for making art and if so can you tell us how?

. . . .

. . . .

- Why do you think that it is important to have art at school?

. . . .

. . . .

- Finally, using whatever materials you have available such as pencil, biro, felt tips, coloured pencils etc., create a self-portrait from memory in the frame below.

References

Booth, T., Ainscow, M., Black-Hawkins, K., Vaughan, M. and Shaw, L. (2000) *Index for Inclusion*. Bristol: CSIE.

DES (1978) *The Warnock Report*. London: DES.

DfEE/QCA (1999) *The National Curriculum Handbook for Secondary Teachers in England and Wales*. QCA/99/458.

DfES (2001) The Revised Special Educational Needs Code of Practice. London: DfES.

DfES (2003) *SEN: Training Materials for the Foundation Subjects*. London: DfES.

DfES (2004) *Removing Barriers to Achievement: The Government's Strategy for SEN*. London: HMSO.

HMSO (1996) Education Act 1996. London: HMSO.

HMSO (2001) The Special Educational Needs and Disability Act (SENDA). London: HMSO.

Ofsted (2003) *Special Educational Needs in the Mainstream*. London: Ofsted.

QCA (2002) Revised National Curriculum.

Stakes, R. and Hornby, G. (2000) *Meeting Special Needs in Mainstream Schools: A Practical Guide for Teachers*. London: David Fulton Publishers.

QCA/ACE (2000) *From Policy to Partnership*. London: QCA/Arts Council for England.